Elephant Bones
and Lonelyhearts

Elephant Bones
and Lonelyhearts

CONFESSIONS ALONG
MY NATURE TRAIL

Ronald Rood

Illustrations by *Larry*
[TERENCE PARKES]

The Stephen Greene Press

BRATTLEBORO • Vermont 05301

This book has been produced in the United States of America and is designed by R. L. Dothard Associates.

It is published by The Stephen Greene Press, Brattleboro, Vermont 05301.

LIBRARY OF CONGRESS CATALOGING IN PUBLICATION DATA

Rood, Ronald N
  Elephant bones and lonelyhearts.

  Includes index.
  1. Nature. 2. Country life—Vermont. 3. Rood, Ronald N. I. Title.
QH81.R736   974.3'5'04   77-79291

ISBN 0-8289-0317-4

Contents

To our friends in the fifty-cents-per-year aggregation known as the Vergennes Forest and Field Club—and especially to Edith and Raymond Slack, who might have saved us that trip to the museum: this book is dedicated to you. You had it coming.

A merry heart doeth good like a medicine.
PROVERBS 17:22

1. *Neighboring*

When we got that station wagon, we discovered we'd also acquired a whole new host of friends.

Not people hoping for a ride, however. People who were suffering from an optical illusion. Or at least a case of mistaken identity.

It seems that, in a small township like ours, you wave at the car as much as you wave at who's in it. From afar you can spot the two-tone pattern, say, that tells you it's Ray Grimes's little Chevvy. Thus you raise a companionable hand in greeting as it draws near. That big Cadillac bearing down on you must be Dan Steadman, and the clatter behind you has got to be Fred Jackman's service truck with its tanks of L–P gas clanging against each other.

In our case we happened to buy a van-type station wagon that was a dead ringer for one owned by Roger Reynolds at the other end of town. So the Reynolds's friends waved at us, while ours waved at them. This went on for weeks until little details such as number plates, radio antennas and differences in the dust jobs told us apart.

As soon as Janice got her driver's license we underwent much closer scrutiny. You could just see our daughter's teenage friends wondering how they should greet the car as we drove through town. If it was Peg or me at the wheel, we'd collect a polite wave. But when Janice drove, other cars would toot, other teenagers would shout a greeting—and Jan would reply in kind. The same happened as Tom, Alison and Roger attained the driving age. Riding with them was like a triumphal return from the wars.

That's the way it is in the country. A neighbor a mile away in a rural area may be much more important to you than the dweller in the next apartment in the city. Peg and I have probably not spoken a hundred words to Charles and Ilene Buss in all the years we've been in Vermont, because they live in a remote part of town. Their farm is well known for its picturesque setting, however, so we understand at once when we hear that something happened "up by Charlie's." And as George and Ruth Strickholm arrived fifteen years ago with half a dozen horses, a passion for hiking, and boundless enthusiasm for both that caught up half the kids in town, many of us are apt to date events as "before Strickholms" or after.

I'm sure some of our neighbors reckon time as before Roods and after, too. Peg and I came to Lincoln along with Dotty and Al Thergesen and a total of six offspring—four of ours and two of theirs. Such an assemblage, arriving with two large moving vans and settling in together on the old Lathrop farm up the river, was bound to be noticed.

We didn't know a soul in town. The only persons we knew in all Vermont were the former owners of our land plus the real estate agent who'd brought us together. We had gotten

RONALD ROOD

tired of New York suburb life, had quit our jobs at a small college at the end of the school year—me as a biology instructor, Al in public relations. Then we checked the real estate ads, and found a home we liked in Lincoln—simple as that. Young and ready for anything, we were scarcely concerned that we had no jobs waiting for us here in the Green Mountains. After all, Al Thergesen had worked as a cabinetmaker and his wife had been a typist. Peg had studied accounting, and I could work as a teacher or salesman or both. We'd get by, we told ourselves. No doubt about it.

No doubt in our minds, at least. But our neighbors were not so sure. In spite of the Vermonter's belief in minding one's own business, here were two families from "down country" who needed a little encouragement. Or so those good people thought. This was a few years after the close of World War II, and many little towns found themselves being deserted as people flocked to the city. Anyone who ran counter to that flow was welcome indeed.

After all, the ten of us *did* represent one-fortieth of the entire population of Lincoln ("Four hundred people, counting women and children," the Town Report stated). Then, too, Louie Lathrop had been a respected member of the community and it seemed good to have his farm occupied once more. Besides, with all those kids we had an interest in the school and the church, so we jumped right into the middle of half the affairs of the town.

Thus we found ourselves on the outskirts of Lincoln, but in the center of its life. The famed coldness of the New Englander was nowhere to be seen. One after another, in the beginning from curiosity but soon out of a genuine interest in our survival, the townspeople indulged themselves in the time-honored practice of "neighboring."

Phil and Maria Heubel were the first. "We know you're not even unpacked," they apologized upon driving into our yard a couple of days after we arrived, "but we're leaving for Germany tomorrow. It looks as if you've got a few mouths to feed. Why don't you help yourselves to our garden while we're gone?"

We jumped at the chance. They were in Europe several weeks—all the way from the early peas to the midseason corn. Yet when they entered our yard they hadn't even learned our names. However, when they had first moved into town, they had been warmly welcomed by their neighbors, so they passed the favor along to us.

A few days later I happened to mention their good deed to Earl Carpenter, who ran the general store. "We have no garden yet," I said to him, "but the Heubels are letting us use theirs."

"Oh?" said Earl. "You know how to care for a garden?"

I told him I'd been raised on a little farm in Connecticut, that we had always grown much of our own food, and would do so even now if I only had a garden. This, I figured, was the end of the conversation.

And indeed it was. Until the following spring, that is. Then, one day, the old plank bridge in front of our home rumbled an announcement of impending company. We could hear the thump of horses' hoofs, the squeak of wheels. Looking out, we saw two horses pulling a farm wagon. In the wagon was a plow. Sitting on the wagon seat was a balding farmer and his graying wife.

"We're here for your garden," the man said simply. "Where do you want it put?"

We hastily picked out a spot handy to the house where there'd be plenty of sun and the soil was well drained. Then we helped unload the plow. Dan Chatfield—for that turned out to be his name—hitched up the two horses and set to work. Soon, while the kids stared in wonder, the rich, fragrant soil was curling away from the shining steel of the plow. Dan, absorbed in his task, scarcely glanced at me. Now and again he spoke a word to those horses as the garden appeared in the meadow, furrow by furrow.

Peg took Carrie Chatfield into the house. They came back half an hour later with snacks and coffee. I held up a coffee

cup, but Dan shook his head. Then I waved a sandwich at
him. "Roast beef," I called.

Dan turned the horses at the end of the furrow. Then he
stopped. "What'd you say?"

When I repeated myself, he dropped the reins and strode
over to us. "Horses all tuckered out—they need a breather.
Roast beef, you say?"

Soon he was back at work—after the horses had suitably
rested. While he finished the job, Carrie gave us a mini-course
on Lincoln. She told of its history, its weather, its people, the
towns that surrounded it, the river that ran through it. She
knew how we could get a plumber ("but better order him
now if you want him before Christmas"). She revealed what
stores in Bristol had the fairest prices and the best merchandise,
where we could get the car serviced and where we couldn't.
In fact, considering the conveyance she'd arrived in, and the
fund of knowledge she imparted, I figured we'd been favored
by a visit from the real Welcome Wagon itself. All others
were nothing but imitations.

The garden took a couple of hours to plow. Dan returned
by himself a day or so later with a harrow to break up the
clumps—and that same afternoon our first seeds were in the
ground.

So we met Dan and Carrie Chatfield. And so, too, began
two-plus decades of friendly treatment at the hands of those
surprising Vermonters. Peg will not soon forget the time she
entered a kitchen in mid-morning, for instance. The man of
the house had returned from his morning chores and was having one of those sumptuous farm breakfasts. Seated at the
table, he pushed a chair out, indicated that she take a seat,
tipped his hat, and went back to his meat and potatoes without
a word. Nor will I forget the lady who materialized in our
driveway one summer's day with a quart of heavy cream. "I
just hope in all this heat it ain't turned ransom," was her only
comment.

The cream, of course, was far from "ransom." Sweet and

Neighboring   11

yellow, it was so thick we had to spoon it from the jar. Her warmth and friendliness came naturally to country life where your neighbor is like a member of your family, even if you live miles apart.

Such was the case when Neil Frink and I first met on a gravel road. The road was ordinarily wide enough for two cars to meet and pass each other with little trouble. On this occasion, however, a late-winter thaw had reduced it to the consistency of an African waterhole. When Neil and I approached each other, we both pulled out to the side. Then, safely by, we both pulled back into the road.

Or so it was planned. However, the whole roadbed was soft, and my right wheel caught in the sloping shoulder. Down went the car, like a foundering ship, up to the axles in mud.

When you pass each other that way on a country road, you check your rearview mirror to see if the other car is all right. Neil saw my predicament and stopped. The next half-hour we maneuvered in the mire. We put sticks and stones under the wheels, driving ahead stick by stick. Slowly we inched toward the center of the road, sometimes slipping back so as to lose all we had gained.

At last I was back in the comparative good driving of the middle of the road. Reaching into my pocket with my two cleanest fingers, I pulled out my wallet, but Neil raised a muddy hand.

"No, thanks," he said. "You don't owe me a thing. This time it was you. Next time it'll probably be me."

That's how it is in these weather-beaten hills. You join forces to achieve a common goal. One blustery day Barbara Woelhaf struggled out through the snow to feed her horse. When she got to the barn she discovered that the doors had blown open, front and back, and the horse had wandered off down the road. Hastening to the car, which hadn't been running for a couple of days, she tried to start it. It sputtered and died, so she turned to her neighbors for help.

Major's tracks showed that he had headed south, doubtless

RONALD ROOD

goaded by the bitter north wind at his rear. Barbara phoned Fletcher and Hattie Brown at the next farm, but they saw no sign of the horse—only his tracks, still headed south. So she called the farm farthest away on the road. Had Major or his tracks been past there yet?

No, they hadn't. "But I can hear the snowplow coming," Helen Clark told her. "When they get here I'll have Carl ask them if they've seen your horse along the way."

Barbara thanked her and hung up. She made a couple of other fruitless calls, then went out to try to start the car again. She was still trying when she heard the approaching racket of the plow. Going to the road, she waited to ask if they had any news for her.

The moment the plow came around the curve she had her answer. Trotting along in front, head held high, steam blowing from his nostrils and obviously enjoying his own little parade, pranced her wayward steed.

When they got to her mailbox, the plow stopped. Major obligingly turned into the driveway and ran right to the barn. "We found him down by the old Baslow place," called the driver. "So Calvin got out, rounded him up, and we herded him home for you."

Nodding in response to her thanks, he stepped on the gas and clattered off down the road in a dramatic whirl of powdered snow.

When you band together like that, you're all on a first-name basis. You're just Howard and Cal and Barbara—a casual little detail, or lack of detail, which we find refreshing. There's scarcely room for fancy veneer when you've got a dead battery, your car has skidded off an icy curve, or you find a storm-tossed tree across your road. Everybody pitches in.

One time Peg was headed for Montpelier on an icy morning. She had her choice: go around by way of the little town of Richmond, or take a chance going straight over a mountain road with a high gap that would save her about twenty miles. The snow tires were good and the scenery should be spectacular in that craggy pass, so she chose the mountain.

As she neared the gap she overtook a line of cars. They had come to a stop behind some unseen stalled vehicle up ahead.

Knowing she'd be in the same fix as they if she slowed down, she made a quick decision. Hoping she could squeeze in between a couple of those inert cars if she met another vehicle coming down, she pulled out around the last car in line without slackening speed. Then she continued up the hill.

She made it almost to the gap. There, just a hundred yards from the top, was the cause of it all: a car that had skidded sideways. Abandoned by its disgusted driver, it had blocked the car in back of it, and the dozen or so cars behind that. Peg managed to fishtail past it, but in so doing lost her forward momentum. And there she came to a halt, first in line and going nowhere.

The people in the other cars doubtless noted her comeuppance with satisfaction. But Peg hadn't finished. Most of Vermont's tricky hills have barrels of sand by the side of the road for just such an occasion. Sometimes the barrel boasts an old shovel; sometimes not. There were two barrels here with plenty of sand but no way to spread it. So Peg opened the back of the station wagon, took out the shovel that Vermonters carry during the winter months, and threw sand under the wheels.

The people in the other cars watched for a moment. None

RONALD ROOD

of them apparently was a Vermonter; at least nobody had thought of the sand. However, they began to rummage around in their own trunks. Not a one of those dozen or so cars had the vital shovel, but they came forth with substitutes: pieces of cardboard, hub caps, even a flattened beer can. Soon the whole crowd had emptied those barrels and had skidproofed the last hundred feet up to the gap.

Anyone who's faced the problem probably knows what they did next. Peg had done it before, so she tried to now: she asked five or six people to get in the back of the station wagon and ride on the bumper. This gave extra traction to the rear wheels, and she went up over the top as if it had been a summer's day.

She told me about it when she got back that evening. "And you know," she said, "they probably got every car moving. I watched a couple of the other cars just out of curiosity. The whole gang would get on the bumper and sit in the trunk. This would give the wheels enough traction to get to the sanded stretch. Then they'd finish the climb without any trouble."

And the abandoned car that had caused it all? "We'd have moved him up first if we could. But I guess he didn't want any help. He'd locked the car—and taken the keys!"

Country-style togetherness works night and day. Sometimes it even catches you napping. One crystal winter night the telephone rang. Groping in the dark, I found the light switch and lifted the receiver. "Hate to bother you at three A.M.," said the caller, "but you'd better take a look outside at the northern lights."

I recognized the voice of Donald Brown. Don suffers from spinal trouble, and, often sleepless, prowls around long after his family is in bed. Thus he'd happened to notice that the room was lighted as if by a full moon—but no moon was to be seen. Going to the window, he'd spotted long luminous rays, as of a dozen searchlights, vaulting up toward the zenith from the northern horizon.

After waking his family, he proceeded to dial a few of his

friends. I'm glad I was in that favored circle. It was the greatest display of the aurora borealis I had seen south of the arctic regions. In addition to the searchlight rays, there were sheets of light that seemed to hang in folds like gigantic curtains. The aurora overspread the entire sky, even to the southern horizon, while patches of red appeared east and west. Flickering pulses played over the whole scene. Sometimes these pulses sprang from behind the mountains to our north and east like faint greenish flames, and other times they danced around the only spot that was dark—a tiny circle of sky almost directly overhead.

Now it was our turn to spread the news. Taking the telephone out onto our front deck so I could watch uninterrupted, I awakened more than a dozen people. Doubtless they, in turn, called others. By three-thirty or four o'clock, half of Lincoln

RONALD ROOD

and the adjoining towns must have been shivering in the ten-degree chill, gawking at the silent fireworks, and saying to themselves as they considered who'd awakened them, "Well—what else are friends for?"

What else, indeed, if not for sharing? We talked about that aurora for days. We remarked how there were no shadows as the light came from everywhere; how a couple of cameras had captured little more than a dim sky, above a silhouette horizon, as the lights had moved throughout the time exposure; how radio and television reception had been erratic the night before. This last was apparently because of the sunspot activity that triggers such an electromagnetic "storm" many miles above the earth, causing gas molecules to glow like those in a neon sign.

A display of northern lights is but one of the many seasonal events that keeps you in touch with your neighbor. One favorite topic, of course, is the weather. The cold becomes a personal thing when it's twenty-five below zero. The chill strikes through a tiny chink like a driven nail. Wall switches grow whiskers of frost because there's scanty insulation between their junction boxes and the external siding. The trees in the woods behind the house snap like pistols as the moisture in their trunks turns to ice.

Clark Atkins gets more business for his little garage than he would prefer on such bitter mornings. He drives from one house to another to "jump-start" cars with his heavy battery cables. And, always, in the Lincoln General Store somebody comes out with the question that makes it sound as if it's all your fault: "Well—is it cold enough for you?"

Never, of course, does the weather become so foul that someone cannot make a joke about it. Old Vern James, who used to live in a little house near the New Haven River, had a huge thermometer on the door of his barn. We used to call it a winter thermometer: it apparently existed to put all lesser thermometers to shame when it came to chilly temperatures. If other people's reading was twenty below zero, say, Vern's would register minus thirty. And there were always a few mornings each winter when he'd answer the inevitable question with a shrug.

" 'How cold was it?' " he'd repeat after the asker. "I don't know. Couldn't read the mercury; it was clear down into the bulb."

One morning, however, the rural mail carrier saw his chance. As he slowed to put some mail in Vern James's box he saw Vern digging and searching in the snow beneath that celebrated thermometer.

"Whatcha doing, Vern?" he shouted. "Looking for your mercury?"

Then, too, I remember Fletcher Brown's comment as he was holding his little grandson, Mike. "How old are you, anyway, Fletcher?" he was asked.

"Twenty-six," was the reply.

"Oh, go on. With a grandson? You're a heck of a lot older than that!"

"Well, I'm really fifty-two. But I've been froze up half my life."

But it remained for old Clint Pierce to put our Vermont weather into perspective. He owned the other store in the village, a tiny market the size of a two-car garage. When Mahlon

RONALD ROOD

Culver complained about the weather one snowy day, Clint set him to rights. "You don't like the weather, Mahlon," he said, "because you don't want to pay the fiddler."

" 'Pay the fiddler'?"

"Sure. Think of the wonderful summers we have around here. The way I figure it, winter in Vermont is the price you pay for summer in Vermont."

He was right on both counts. The summers are idyllic, at least most of the time. However, we tend to forget one season when we're steeped in another. So impressive are those wintry days that the brief summer seems like just a pause between frosts. As one hard-bitten resident observed, Vermont has eleven months of snow and one month of tough sledding.

That elusive summer takes place sometime after "mud time," that fifth season whose delights I've already mentioned. Doubtless one cause of the summer's briefness is the grip that winter maintains on the land. The severity of the cold is closely related to the amount of snow on the ground. Although the temperature may plummet to minus thirty degrees Fahrenheit on a bitter night, the earth under a single foot of fluffy snow may be just at freezing temperature—a gradient of sixty degrees.

With good snow cover, the ground may freeze to only a few inches. Sometimes, if the snow arrives early and stays all winter, the ground scarcely freezes at all. With an "open winter," however, the exposed earth may become rock-hard to a depth of three feet. Then, with spring thaws, we get a whopper of a mud season.

Farmers find it almost impossible to get on their fields with machinery when all that ground is thawing. Maple-sugar makers, enjoying easy access to tap their trees while the ground is frozen and snowless, may find a disappointing season. Ideally, maple sap production depends on warm spring days and freezing nights, but without the steadying influence of a layer of snow in the woods, the ground may thaw too rapidly for a good sap flow.

Neighboring   19

"Oh, well," the sugar maker says as he surveys his diminished crop, "short and sweet. You can't do much of anything else in mud season, anyway."

The mud dries up sometime in late April or early May. Mary Pierce removes the log that has blocked her driveway. The log is not some kind of unwelcome mat; it merely keeps unwary visitors from entering and sinking to the gunwales. It also saves the complexion of her driveway. Bessie Pixley puts the first peas in the soil ("I gamble on the chance they'll grow in the cold and wet. Seed's cheap, anyway; if they don't sprout I can plant again."). Harold Masterson goes past the house several times daily on his tractor, driving between the scattered fields he's farming. The country air is redolent with the fragrance of newly manured land. Mud season is past, and summer is poised.

Spring gets sandwiched in there somewhere, it is true. It is a short season at best. Although some spring flowers had begun back in March with the appearance of the first pussy willows, most of them have to wait awhile. The ground must warm before they can do much serious growing. The daily thaw-freeze-thaw routine may be great for stimulating sap flow in the maples, but it's an effective damper on the activities of the smaller plants.

When balmy weather finally arrives for good, the effect on the plants is astonishing. You can practically hear them grow. With apparent high exuberance they change stored starch in roots or seeds to the sugary raw material to make new leaves, stems, flowers. Water absorbed from the soil builds tissues almost while you watch.

Small plants on the forest floor are especially adept at this annual spring sprint. They have to be; when the leaves of the trees close the canopy overhead, they'll be plunged into shade. So the hepaticas, violets, trout lilies, spring beauties, trilliums and lady's-slippers join the hundreds of other green opportunists. Together they get a jump on the season.

Dandelions and wild mustards in the fields, marsh marigolds

RONALD ROOD

in the swamps, and native strawberries on the hillsides race against time, too. They open their petals almost frantically to gain the attention of bees and other insects before the shrubs and tall grasses blanket the area. It's a buoyant and colorful race, yes—but also a desperate one.

The passing parade of plants is marked by my neighbors. Much of the life of the country is determined by the weather. Country-dwellers often take their cues for planting, harvesting, and other outdoor activities from observations of plants and animals.

A common white-flowered little tree known scientifically as Amelanchier, for instance, blooms during a definite few days in spring. At one time the Indians—and, later, the colonists—could figure out when the fish known as shad was running upstream into the rivers to spawn: the white-flowered tree was in bloom. The tree became known as shadblow, shadplum, or simply as shad, after the tasty fish whose fortunes—or misfortunes—were so closely allied with its own reproductive cycle.

Today the fish is of less importance. Anyway, we do not need a shrubby tree to tell when it's running—newspapers and radio do the job. Shadblow still fits in the scheme of things, however. "Don't count on green grass in the pasture," a farmer told us when we wondered how soon we could turn our family cow out to forage for herself, "until after shadblow's done."

Corn, it seems, should not be planted until the buds of hickory trees are as large as a crow's beak. Old-timers were familiar with crows and hickories; both are still fairly well known in the country. The hickory possesses one of the largest buds. The bud swells to about the size of the last two joints of your little finger just when the weather will probably remain warm enough to allow tender corn shoots to escape any late frost.

Do you want to know when to plant your cucumbers? "Wait 'til after lilac time," advises a neighbor. In Lincoln, this would place it around the end of the first week in June, when

Neighboring 21

the lilac blooms have nearly run their course. Wise counsel, too; our last frost generally occurs around the second of June.

The phases of the moon are also important. That potential frost toward the first of June often occurs when the moon is full. The last full moon before the official start of autumn may likewise bring a dip in temperatures. Sometimes it occurs as early as August twenty-fifth. If you're familiar with the shocking change over the countryside after a killer frost has blackened thousands of plants, you know that, in the country, the moon represents much more than a romantic light in the sky.

The moon is also responsible, in a way, for the size of the congregation on Easter morning here in Lincoln. The date of Easter Sunday, as is well known, varies by nearly a month from year to year. Actually, the date is established by the phases of the moon. It harkens back to an early pagan ritual dedicated to Oestrus, the goddess of spring. When the early Christians wanted to set an annual observance of the Resurrection, they found a ready-made celebration waiting. And so Oestrus, or Easter, occurs in accordance with a complex but venerable timetable. It falls on the first Sunday after the first full moon following March 21—the first day of spring.

And now for the change in church attendance. Maple-sugar making is very much a part of my adopted little town. Those apparently slumbering trees are likewise sensitive to the phases of the moon. A full moon often means that the buckets are full on the trees or the modern pipeline is delivering a steady stream to the holding tank. Hence, more often than not, the ranks of the Easter celebrants are thinned a bit because of what's going on in the adjoining wooded slopes: sap's running and there's boiling to be done.

"There's always sugaring on Easter," Deacon Fletcher Brown told me on such a morning. "Hattie and I made it here to church, but we can't stay around and visit. Those tanks and buckets are running over. I can hear them clear down here—a mile away." And with that he and his wife fled to their waiting Jeep.

RONALD ROOD

Summer's plans are often laid according to the moon and the weather, too. A ring around the moon is usually an indication of impending rain. The wider the ring, the farther away the weather change will be. The ring is actually caused by clouds of vapor or frost high in the air. In summer the moon is "taking a bath" on such an occasion; in winter it's wading in a snowdrift.

Red sky at night is a sailor's delight, according to the old saying, for it indicates a fair day to follow. "Red sky in the morning, sailors take warning," is the other half of this little verse. Here in the hills where sailors are scarce, due notation of such colorful displays has been delegated to farmers. They also watch to see if the grass is wet with a dew in the morning (good weather) or if the grass is dry (approaching rain).

Then, too, if it rains early in the morning, chances are it will stop by noon. "Rain before seven, clear before eleven," my friends assure themselves as they consider the possibility of getting hay in, cultivating crops or spraying the apples. They also watch the actions of chickens and turkeys when it begins to rain. If the birds run for cover, it's a brief wetting; if they nonchalantly go about their business, it'll probably rain all day. If you think about such antics a moment, they sound backward. But then, what's logic to a chicken?

The coming of weather fronts is usually heralded by freshening winds. Such winds, borne well above the earth, encounter the side of a mountain before they affect the lower valleys. The forested slopes of Lincoln's Mt. Abraham, several square miles in area, sigh and mutter with these gusts while the town itself still may be in the calm. "When the mountain roars, close your doors," my neighbors say as they prepare for wind and weather.

Clouds, of course, have long been scrutinized for hints as to what the weather will be. My neighbors share the general knowledge that the white, fleecy, woolly-sheep cumulus clouds indicate a good day, while the towering, black cumulonimbus warns "thunderstorm." High, regularly patterned rows of cirrocumulus clouds are known as "mackerel sky" after a resemblance to the design scheme on the side of the fish of the same name. They usually precede wet weather. "A mackerel sky will never go dry," the folks at the general store agree.

Now they even scout the trails left by high-flying jets. A plane's vapor trail contains particles of moisture. If the trail evaporates or fades rapidly, the air is dry. If the trail hangs for a long time and even enlarges until it makes a broad band from one horizon to the other, it has served as a nucleus on which further moisture has condensed. Such moisture-laden air is likely to cloud up and rain, whether an airplane triggers it or not. This cause-and-effect sequence was pointed out to me by the patriarch of the town, Otto Butterfield, when I asked him what he thought the weather would be for the weekend.

"Rainy," was his reply.

"How do you know?" I said, expecting to hear something about his arthritis acting up, how the birds were flying low, or the cattle switching their tails—all three signs of an ill wind, by the way.

In reply, he raised his eyes to a pair of rapidly widening white streamers in the sky.

"Jets told me," he said.

Otto's wife, Lizzie, no slouch as a prognosticator herself, gave me the weather report on another occasion as I stood in her doorway and looked out at a drizzly street. "Is it ever going to stop raining?" I asked.

For answer, Lizzie poked her head out past me. Squinting at the sky for a moment, she blinked as the rain spattered on the doorjamb beside her. Then, withdrawing, she faced me with a twinkle that wasn't entirely caused by the raindrops on her face.

"Well, Ron," she said slowly, "it always has."

Weather predictions, and similar banter, even of Lizzie Butterfield's tongue-in-cheek variety, are not lightly shared with just anybody. You have to earn them somehow. In our case, the interest we had in community affairs doubtless helped toward our being accepted. Of course, we had more than an idle concern, with a total of six kids in school. Then, too, Dotty and Al Thergesen, Peg and I all liked music. We formed a vocal quartet that gave programs at various meetings in our section of the state, thus enabling us to get acquainted. So, in a matter of a few months, we found ourselves with a host of good friends.

How good, none of us dreamed. But one March morning after Al had gone to work and I was putting the finishing touches on the chores, Aleta Thergesen came running out to the barn.

"Quick!" she screamed. "Oh, quick! Something has happened to Mommy!"

Racing to the house with her, I found our small son, Tom, standing wide-eyed in the living room. Wordlessly he pointed up the stairs.

Taking the steps in great leaps, I arrived at the Thergesens' bedroom. Dotty lay on the floor. Peg was positioning her for artificial respiration.

"She just dropped," my wife said. "One minute she was making the bed and then she just dropped."

Scarcely believing what was happening, I knelt beside Peg. I had taken a lifesaving course in the service; now I prayed I'd remember how to proceed. "I'll do it, Peg," I told her. "You see that her mouth is clear. Then call the doctor."

Bending to the task, I placed my hands on her lower ribs. Then I started in earnest what I had practiced so many times: "Out goes the bad air . . . in comes the good . . . out goes the bad air . . . " Down and up, down and up, twelve times a minute.

On and on I went, for what seemed the rest of the morning. Not once did I take my eyes from that ash-gray face. Why didn't her eyelids flicker, her lips move?

But there was no sign.

Peg had taken the four younger children downstairs while

she made the phone call. Our elder daughter, Janice, stood numbly with Aleta Thergesen while I pushed and relaxed, pushed and relaxed: Out goes the bad air . . . in comes the good . . .

Then I heard a car in the yard. The front door opened and in a moment Dr. Shepard entered the room.

Stethoscope in hand, he knelt beside me. While I continued in my desperate seesaw, he listened intently. Then he placed a hand on my shoulders.

"You can rest now," he said. "She's gone."

Wearily I let my arms fall to my side. Almost uncomprehending, I remained kneeling and looking at her. I was still kneeling when Al burst through the door.

Our silence told him all he needed to know. Throwing himself on the body of his wife, he sobbed in anguish. "She's still warm!" he cried.

But his despair was to no avail. Al Thergesen had lost his wife. Aleta and Gayle had lost their mother. Peg and I had lost a dear friend.

Almost instantly, however, new friends came to the Thergesens' side. The passage of the ambulance had been noted from one end of town to the other. A little telephoning among neighbors soon established where it must have stopped. Within an hour or so the news was widespread, and those good Vermonters showed what friends they really were.

They came by pickup truck, Jeep and car. The Martells dropped by in their only conveyance—a horse-drawn buggy. Some visitors had obviously dropped their work on the farm and had hastened to visit a neighbor in need. Others were washed and shaven and clean. One farmer, complete with quid of tobacco, sat and looked around uneasily until Peg supplied an old can as a makeshift cuspidor.

At such a time just the presence of your friends is a comfort. However, these friends did not stop there. Their companionship continued long after they were gone, for they had brought enough food for a week. Casseroles, homemade pies

RONALD ROOD

and cake, fragrant loaves of still-warm bread, beans baked in Vermont maple syrup—all were the best efforts of these wonderful people who shared our loss in their wonderful way.

Nor was that all. Dotty's former home was in Reading, Pennsylvania, and she was to be buried there. "I'll milk the cow while you're gone," Norm Lafayette stated. "Martyn and I will take charge of the kids," said Vivian Hutchins. "We'll farm 'em out around town. Just hope you get them all back."

Winston and Daisy Farr promised to check the house daily to be sure the heat stayed on and the pipes didn't freeze on one of those early March nights. Fletcher Brown volunteered to plow the driveway in case there was a snow. Clayt and Zelva Ladeau made up a huge basket of fruit to take to Dotty's parents. Earl Carpenter shrugged when I went to give him the money for the tankful of gas I put in the car on our way out of town. "It's already been paid," he said.

So they stood beside us, those incredible neighbors, all the way to Pennsylvania. When we returned they were right at hand, too. There was a dish of Hungarian goulash in the refrigerator, plus a pie and fresh sweet rolls; and the cow's latest offerings of milk were there, with a note telling that she'd been fed and milked for the day.

One brief mention, by the way, of the neighbors we met in Reading. Or, more correctly, didn't meet. Dotty's parents had lived in the same suburban duplex apartment house for five years; the other half of the house had been occupied by another couple nearly as long. There were two similar houses across the street. When any of them chanced to meet while taking in the paper or putting out the garbage, they'd nod and perhaps share a brief comment on the weather. And now, with all the activities that obviously centered around a death in the family, how did this little neighborhood react?

It didn't. At least, not in the three days we were there. There were still the same polite nods, the same observations about the weather as always. And yet we know that those apartment-dwellers, given half a chance to come out of their protective shells, would doubtless be the same warm, friendly people we had left back in supposedly cold, inhospitable Vermont. But that's what the city does to you.

That is what the country does to you, too. You line up together to defeat whatever the enemy may be at the moment: a blizzard, a crop failure, a burned-out barn, a family tragedy. Only when things are going unusually—almost uncannily—well do you have merely a nodding acquaintance with people who share the same valley, the same general store, the same clouds and the same rural mail carrier. You may be too busy at the moment to stop for a chat, but that's only a temporary condition.

One story has it that a certain man entered the country store, bought a few groceries, and left with only a pleasant "Good morning!" to some of his cronies in the store.

Two of the patrons looked after his car as it drove out of sight. "Huh!" said one. "Wonder what ails *him* today?"

So neighboring, as once practiced by much of humankind, still exists in little pockets here and there. It springs from genuine interest and concern, plus a need to share the good and the bad. After all, we're not only social creatures, but sociable ones as well.

If Fred Pierce's house burns to the ground (which it did) the town turns out to build him a new one (which it did). If Fred Pixley takes an emergency trip to the hospital and his friends learn about it in church on Sunday morning, they'll get up an impromptu purse and handwritten card between the first hymn and the benediction—no matter what it does to the Reverend Terry Cutler's sermon. And on the days just before Christmas, Bill McKean, the aforementioned rural mail carrier, ends up with nearly as many packages in his Jeep at the end of his rounds as when he began his deliveries. Packages like homemade fudge, for instance, or a venison mince pie, or a hand-knit woolen scarf with BILL worked into the pattern. That's what they think of *him*.

By the way, the concern of our neighbors continued after

Al and the kids were back together following Dotty's heart attack. Agnes and Barton Van Vliet, friends in the neighboring town of Bristol, learned about a girl who had lost her husband. They determined that if Al could meet her, perhaps two shattered families might be mended.

Matchmaking is, of course, nothing new. However, it was the manner of the match that was interesting. The idea was to have Al and Norene meet in one of the most favorable of all atmospheres: the time-honored potluck dinner. In this dinner, everyone brings a hot or cold dish, salad or dessert and puts it on a huge table. Then the participants all sample this somewhat impromptu smorgasbord. It's a rural buffet *au jus*—or *au naturel*—in all its native flavor.

Some of the best meals in this country, I'm convinced, are found at potluck dinners even if you do occasionally bump into eighteen salads and only three desserts, as happened once at an outdoor beanbake in Lincoln.

The dinner was to be a late-summer picnic. The whole town was invited. Al and Norene were both told the other would be present—and they were to take it from there.

It worked like a movie. Some eighty people showed up.

Neighboring

Under the salubrious influence of a dozen kinds of breads, an equal number each of salads, main dishes and desserts, plus home-cranked ice cream, what else could Al and Norene say to each other?

And so Gayle and Aleta Thergesen soon had a new mother, while Joan Denny got a new father. They moved from Vermont to Al's boyhood home in Connecticut—and the story had its happy ending.

It was against the backdrop of such personal care and interest, plus the incredible blue of the Vermont sky, the green of its mountains and the whiteness of its winters, that we chose to raise our four children. It was there, too, that an opportunity arose to embark on a career I'd always admired in others, but never thought I could pursue myself: the craft of writing.

The Lincolnites were concerned about my new pursuit, as well. Doubtless they thoughtfully considered this turn of events on the old Louis Lathrop farm, but only later did I realize *how* they considered it.

In the meantime, Peg and I congratulated ourselves on our new-found friends. There weren't any movie houses or restaurants in Lincoln, true. There weren't even any street lights other than half a dozen right in the center of town. But it really didn't matter. Down the valley, up through the woods, and over by Charlie's, we had lots of neighbors.

To the Lincolnites, the whole Green Mountain State was wrapped up in their little town. As an elderly lady known by nearly everybody as Granny once confided in me: "I was never out of Vermont but once. And that was to Bennington." Which, in case you're not up on your Vermont geography, is only a hundred miles away in the southwest corner of the state.

Yes, we had everything that was necessary. Even, as I said at the beginning, a car that's a twin to somebody else's. Thus there's no need to try to keep up with the Joneses. In a small town like ours, you *are* the Joneses. So are all the other people, too.

2. *"Since You Don't Work, Ron —"*

"Janice, what does your father do?"

My elder daughter was at a dance at the University of Vermont. To make conversation, her date inquired about her home and her family. Hence the question about my occupation.

"Oh," said Janice, "he's a naturalist."

There was a long silence. The boy was obviously thinking about what she'd said. Then, at last, he brought his thoughts out into the open.

"A naturalist, eh? Even in the winter do they run around like that?"

Not all misunderstandings are as far afield as confusing a

31

naturalist with a nudist. Sometimes people just wonder what I can possibly be doing in the house on the hill. Being a naturalist is a prime occupation for someone who lives on an extinct farm, it seems to me. However, it's not so clear to others. As I hinted at the end of the previous chapter, people gained all sorts of impressions when I turned my efforts to writing.

The chance to write—or, more correctly, to become a naturalist-turned-writer—sort of came in through the woodshed, as my Vermont neighbors might say. After we'd moved up from Long Island and had settled in Lincoln, the immediate question was that of gainful employment. Al Thergesen found a job at a furniture factory while I tried my hand as a salesman for an insulation company headquartered in nearby Barre.

I was a good salesman, too. That is, if by "good salesman" you mean someone who makes house calls. Lloyd Hutchins, owner of the company, assured me that the successful salesman made plenty of contacts. So away I went on my visits. Each day some dozen or so potential customers would learn that I just happened to be in the neighborhood and dropped by to say hello.

We'd talk about the weather, the big fish he'd caught, or the mess at the capitol in Montpelier. I'd admire his dog, his garden, pictures of his children. He'd admire my samples of roofing and siding, and be properly impressed at how warm the insulation was. But when he told me he couldn't afford to spend another dollar, I'd agree with him.

Dolefully my prospect would recite the problems facing him the first of every month. With each grim detail I'd put away another sample. By the time he got to the payments on the speedboat, I wouldn't have a shingle showing. Then, as with all good sales interviews, would come the clincher.

"So you see, Mr. Rood, I'm not in the market just now. But I'll sure keep you in mind."

And away I'd go—sold.

Occasionally I did manage to measure up a few storm windows or get a contract for insulating a house. Since I made plenty of calls, the Laws of Chance were on my side. Especially when I stopped to see Merle Crown.

Merle was the principal of Vergennes Union High School. No, he didn't need any roofing or siding. His windows and insulation were in fine shape, too. "But I tell you what I *do* need, Mr. Rood. We've got a sudden opening for a biology teacher. Know anybody who'd be interested?"

Did I? How loud was Opportunity supposed to knock?

So I retired my samples and tucked away the before-and-after book that showed what siding could do. Then I rejoined the world of the amoeba and the pickled frog. It was great to be in school again—even if all those prospective customers were going to miss me. They'd have to find someone else to talk to about politics and the weather, that's all.

When you teach, you soon get immersed in your subject—that is, if you're trying to do a reasonably good job. You take papers home to correct. You read books and magazines about your specialty. You join professional associations, take evening and summer courses. You go back to the school on Saturday mornings and Sunday afternoons to set up for those kids on Monday. If there ever was a learn-while-you-earn project, it's teaching.

With all this activity there's bound to be some sort of spin-off, or fringe benefit. In my case it was writing. I'd been fascinated with the world of living things ever since my little brother Jim and I had tearfully buried a squashed caterpillar. It was not enough to talk about plants and animals with a hundred biology students daily; I wanted to keep on teaching after that last bell had rung. Writing seemed the logical next step.

This step came about because there seemed to be a real need for it. In the course of lesson plans and lab preparation, I consulted the works of other teachers and biologists. I wanted to see how they had initiated their students into the mysteries of what makes the ivy twine, for instance, or how you can tell the sex of a turtle. Then, too, recalling the old axiom that the only thing certain about a classroom demonstration is that it

"Since You Don't Work, Ron—"

won't work, I wondered if any means had been found to circumvent failure while I'd been away from teaching.

Yes, indeed, there was plenty to read. Much of it was clear and informative and would give valuable outside help to my students in addition to their own text and lab manuals. But some of it, although just as informative, was nowhere near as clear. In fact, it was downright muddy. About the only people who would ever read many of those scientific treatises would be other scientists. Which, to my way of thinking, was a shame: such writing contained fascinating material about an absorbing subject—life itself.

Consider one of the questions I posed a moment ago, for instance: how to tell a male turtle from a female. Not a subject of global impact, perhaps, but one that interests high school sophomores the first time a turtle comes to class. After all, here's a question that concerns sex—and that's a subject that *can* shake the world. Barring the possibility of being born a turtle—in which case you've got the answer—just how do you tell?

See if you can get the clue from this little quote: "The plastron of the male may exhibit a degree of medial concavity, while the caudal extremity is superficially more robust and projects well beyond the cloacal aperture, usually being visible beyond the carapace from above."

Which, in case you missed it, means that the male is hollow-chested and has a longer tail.

Or take the description of a certain object useful to biologists. It has a broad, curved blade, slightly pointed at the end. The blade is attached to a handle in such a way that it may be driven into the ground to remove a scoop of earth. Such an object is familiarly known as a shovel, of course. But not in a geology book in the school library. There it was, its picture solemnly labeled GEOTOME.

"Geotome" does, indeed, mean "shovel" in technical lingo. But why the fancy name? So I decided to serve as a sort of interpreter between science and the general public—from my own students on up. With the raw material of biology all around me during the working day and the lively interest of the students to keep me on my toes, perhaps I could translate perfectly good biological parlance into equally good vernacular. In other words, I'd call a spade a spade.

I had tried my hand at writing once before. When I was teaching on Long Island, Peg and I had moved into a new development in the south shore town of Islip. Ours was the first house made ready for occupancy; the second gained its tenants about a week later. Our new neighbors turned out to be Lawrence Elliott and his wife, Lola.

I thought I had seen Larry's name in print once or twice. When I asked I found he was on the editorial staff of *Coronet* magazine. One day, just to make conversation, I wondered aloud how a person might go about becoming a writer.

"Nothing to it," Larry assured me. "The difference between the writer and the non-writer is that the writer writes. That's all."

Hm–m–m. That didn't sound difficult. Recalling what I'd seen in various papers and magazines, I felt that I could dream up a subject or two, myself. Since everybody knew that writers made good money, I decided to give it a try. Especially with Larry there to lend a hand.

What would I write about? "Write about what you know best," said Larry. "For instance, you like animals. Give me an animal story and I'll take it in to the office."

This was in the spring of 1953. There was an interesting event right at hand: a "hatch" of seventeen-year locusts on the island. After long years of feeding on tree roots, the nymphs had emerged from the ground, each leaving a hole the size of a dime. Climbing trees, telephone poles and buildings, they shed their skins and transformed into winged adults. These adults looked like giant flies as large as the end joint of your thumb. They were present by the millions—crawling, flying and singing their long, high-pitched mating song from dawn until dusk.

I had studied these "locusts"—or, more properly, cicadas—

with my biology classes at the ag school where I taught. We had discovered that, for all their size, they were harmless. True locusts are actually ravenous grasshoppers, but these cicadas did little more than startle people as they crawled over every inch of vegetation and plugged storm sewers with their drowned bodies during a rain. Soon they'd lay eggs, die, and be gone for another seventeen years.

It seemed like a story made to order, so I sat down that evening and wrote it. The next day I gave it to Larry, who took it in for a conference with his fellow editors.

I had the check practically spent in my imagination when Larry materialized at the door one evening. He had a folder in his hand. "Here's your story," he said. "They didn't take it."

I was incredulous. "They didn't?"

"Nope. The boss lives on the north shore and they don't have a single cicada up there. So when you said they were 'everywhere on the island' he found it hard to believe you."

Of course, when one part of a story doesn't ring true, you treat the whole thing with suspicion. I had read everything I could find about the seventeen-year cicada but I had missed that one little point. In spite of numbers so thick that the Long Island Rail Road trains had trouble starting and stopping because of their crushed bodies on the rails, the whole outbreak was strictly local. Automobiles in Islip boiled over because of clogged radiators, while ten miles away—and up on that north shore of Long Island—there were no cicadas at all.

Score one for Larry's boss. As I was new at the game, I didn't recognize that he had taught me a priceless lesson. "Do your homework," he was saying. "And do it well. All of it."

Temporarily stymied, I resolved not to let such a thing happen again. However, before I could dream up something else, we moved from Long Island to Vermont. At the same time Larry left the staff of *Coronet*. "Send them something else, Ron," he wrote to me, "even if I'm no longer there."

His letter was so optimistic that I decided to try again. After all, I was out in the cold now, so I might as well take a chance. What could I lose?

Following Larry's advice, I chose another subject I knew well: the swamps around my boyhood home in Connecticut. The most vocal inhabitant of such swamps was the garrulous little amphibian known as the spring peeper. So small, even when fully grown, that it could sit on your thumbnail with hardly anything hanging over, this tiny frog *surely* must have been noticed even on that vital north shore of Long Island. It bravely chose to sing and cavort and lay eggs while the water was yet ice cold; hence it was a welcome herald of spring.

After snooping into the facts of life of *Hyla crucifer* and satisfying myself that I wasn't making another glaring mistake, I sent the story of this blythe spirit down to *Coronet*.

About two weeks later I got a telephone call. It was Ben Merson, of the editorial staff. They liked the piece, were buying it, "and what are you going to do next for us, Mr. Rood?"

Hastily turning mental flips, I reeled off a few animal names. A couple of them apparently sounded good to him. "Send them in when you can," he said. "And thanks a lot."

They bought it!

As it turned out, I wrote several pieces for the magazine. They were all on my favorite subject: animals. It was fun to study about them, fun to write about them. I might have continued writing for *Coronet* except for one small detail. There was no connection with the quality of my stories, I trust, but in the early 1960's not merely one editor moved away: the whole magazine quit publication.

I had sold them half a dozen articles during those roofing and insulation days, but when *Coronet* folded, so did I. Although the magazine was later revived under different leadership, I didn't recognize the new names on the masthead. Suffering from salesman's slump, perhaps, I was reluctant to try to re-introduce myself. Besides, I argued, they doubtless had plenty of writers. So that ended my relationship with *Coronet*.

Then came that position at the high school. To many of my students biology was a foreign language, even in what I thought was a clearly worded textbook. Sending them off on their own into the wasteland that is professionally known as "the literature" would turn them off completely. So that's where I decided to take up writing again. I could decipher biology for my hundred-plus students in class; then I could go home and do the same for a few hundred thousand more "students" whom I'd never meet.

Remembering what Lloyd Hutchins had said about the good salesman making plenty of contacts, I figured the same would hold true for a good writer. So I set about to blitz the publishing world. Night after night, when the schoolwork was done, I concocted suggestions for article ideas. I sent the ideas to magazines, newspapers, book publishers. These suggestions, known to the trade as queries, went into our rural mailbox as I passed it at the end of the driveway each morning. Home that night, I'd dream up more queries, and so on. All accompanied, in what I hoped was a convincing professional style, by a stamped, self-addressed return envelope.

Some days I'd cast my literary bread on the waters to the tune of half a dozen queries. Other days I'd send out just one —and, during examination or report-card time, none at all. It almost got so the biology class was my second job.

Before long the replies started coming in. Many of them were stiff little slips of paper that began, "Thank you for your recent suggestion. We regret that . . . " Others let me down more easily, with a scribbled note at the bottom. Still others softened the blow with a personal letter. And a few, a very few, told me to give it a go, "on speculation, of course, Mr. Rood." This did not necessarily mean a sale, but at least it meant there would be some editor waiting to read what I'd have to say.

However, there were not only editors Out There. There were also inspectors. No, I should capitalize the word: Inspec-

tors. After all, this bombardment was being leveled from Lincoln, Vermont—not Lincoln, Nebraska, or some equally sizable town. In those impressive places my efforts would, of course, have gone unnoticed. But not in Lindley Bicknell's post office, which was actually the front room of a house. All of a sudden Linny was selling nearly twice as much first-class postage as he'd sold for years—and the then United States Post Office Department wanted to know why.

So up came the Inspector from Washington. Joined by a local dignitary at the airport in Burlington, he materialized in the doorway of that questionable front room in Lincoln. There the two of them commandeered the books. They snooped into past performance, current sales, projected business. This Board of Inquiry analyzed the postal business of the Town of Lincoln, Vermont, almost as if the proceedings were on television.

A lesser man than Lindley Bicknell would have lost his

"Since You Don't Work, Ron—"

stamp pad right there. However, Linny is a Vermonter. Besides, he's a friend of mine. On several occasions I had joyfully burst into that tiny post office, waving a letter of acceptance for him to read, and buying a new sheet of stamps with the anticipated profits. So, as best he could, Linny told the authorities to humor me.

At least partially mollified, the two inspectors stalked out. Each returned to his desk—there, no doubt, to file a pound of reports. And thus was satisfied officialdom's anxiety that there be no suggestion of taint about its operations. Not in the Lincoln post office, at least.

That is how the United States government reacted to my profession. As I've hinted before, my neighbors had their own ideas as well. I learned about them in the process of writing my first book.

The book, *Land Alive*, is a chronicle of the four seasons on this old farm two miles upriver from Lincoln. Its main characters are the plants and animals of our hundred acres of forests and fields. Although I'd been working on the book for some time, I said little about it when people asked me. I didn't want to disappoint anybody in case it fell flat.

One day, while doing research for the book at the Middlebury College library, I realized that I'd be late for supper. Calling Peg on the phone, I told her to go ahead and feed the kids; I'd scrounge up some leftovers when I got home. Then I returned to my studies.

The work was more tedious than I'd planned, however, and I found myself getting glassy-eyed at about six P.M. So I closed the books and headed for home.

Driving from Middlebury to Lincoln, you go through the town of Bristol. As I paused at the town's only traffic light, a poster caught my eye: PUBLIC SUPPER AT THE FEDERATED CHURCH. Since I knew Peg wasn't expecting me, I decided to sample some of that good Vermont cooking. So I turned the car up North Street.

I bought a ticket at the door and headed for the dining room. Spotting a single empty place at a table where there were seven ladies already waiting to be served, I pulled out a chair and sat down.

At once the seven ladies got up and left. "There you go, Stupid," I told myself. "Blundering in where you don't belong. They were probably waiting for Lady Number Eight, and you botched up their seating arrangement."

The ladies alighted at another table while various other people came and sat at mine. I enjoyed a great home-cooked meal, two cups of coffee—and forgot the whole incident.

The months passed, and finally *Land Alive* was published. It had been out several weeks when I happened to meet one of those ladies in the local variety store. "Mr. Rood," she said, "I owe you an apology."

"Really? I don't get many of those. What's this one for?"

"Well, do you remember when you sat down at our table and we all got up and walked away?"

I had forgotten it, but she recited the details until the memory returned. "Oh, that!" I said. "I figured I had taken a seat reserved for somebody else, so you moved to a larger table. Think nothing of it."

"Oh no," she continued. "We *meant* to leave."

"You did?"

"Yes, we did. We all thought you were writing another *Peyton Place*—"

Then came the clincher: "—And we thought we were going to be in it!"

If she hadn't added that last part I might still have forgotten the whole affair. Now, however, whenever I see her I find her much more interesting. Why should she be worried by a possible sequel to that story of scandal in a small town? What are you hiding, Madam, anyway?

That first book apparently found a few friends, even though it may have proved a secret disappointment to the Shaken Seven. It was well enough received to suggest that I try another. My free-lance magazine writing gained momentum, too. There were less "We are sorry" letters; more "We are interested." I could even list my occupation on the income tax form as "writer" if I wished: hadn't the Post Office Department proved that?

Now, however, this created another question. With a second book in the works, magazine articles a-borning and those same hundred biology students thirsting for knowledge, how could one person do it all? You just can't scintillate in front of the class all day and then go home and scintillate on the typewriter all evening. Besides, there was the little matter of four kids and a wife. Something had to give.

Teaching was great; I loved it. But now that I'd gotten a taste of writing I had become fond of that, too. So, feeling that in writing I could continue to follow my aim of bringing science down where people could understand it, I decided to swap permanently those hundred students for what I hoped were thousands. Eyeing that teaching contract with its fifty-two weeks of nice, guaranteed money, I gave it back to the Vergennes school board unsigned.

You don't turn over a steady job for the uncertainties of a

RONALD ROOD

writing career, however. Not just like that, at least. There was a family to support, bills to pay. We couldn't live merely on "We are interesteds," from the first blush of some brilliant idea until it was completed and paid for by the magazine weeks or months later. Somebody had to help us keep ahead of the butcher and the baker and the tax collector. And this is where it helped to have a girl like Peg.

My wife had long been interested in the education of small children. She had majored in child development in college, and had helped in a local nursery school. Perhaps with a sneaky suspicion as to my prowess as a salesman, she had taken enough refresher courses to gain her teaching certificate. Quizzing around in the local towns, she ran into a stroke of luck: the Middlebury school system had an opening.

"Just what I wanted," she told me, waving a letter from the superintendent. "Kindergarten!"

This was perfect, she exulted. She'd always have a parking place in the morning ("They don't have their drivers' licenses yet, do they?"); discipline should be no problem ("I'm bigger than they are"); and she wouldn't have to drag papers home to correct ("How much can a five-year-old write in the time between 'sand box' and 'rest rug,' anyway?").

So, when I decided to take the big step, Peg had already been teaching a couple of years. Now all that remained was for us each to prove to the other that we'd made the right decision—that the whole thing worked. Although Roger, our youngest, was in school now so there were no children at home, we had still reversed the traditional roles of man and woman. I suppose you could say that a decade before her compatriots claimed it was her right, Peg had become liberated: she went out to bring home the bacon while I stayed home and tried for the gravy.

All this required a little explanation in Lincoln. When school opened that first autumn and I didn't make the daily trek to Vergennes as I had done in previous years, it was obvious that

I was no longer working. After all, you go away somewhere to work: anybody knows that. You don't work at home—unless you're a farmer, that is. But there I sat, up at the edge of the woods, apparently without gainful employment—doing nothing at all.

In a large city such seeming hibernation would be dismissed with a shrug. The little village of Lincoln, however, was populated by our friends, not merely by a bunch of strangers. They'd opened their hearts to us that first year when Dotty Thergesen died. They had enjoyed town picnics, softball games and trips to two Worlds Fairs with us. Together we had fought fires, put up a little ski tow in the center of town, built an entire community school without a penny of state or federal aid. Even if they didn't ask it, we felt that such good friends should share in our latest turn of events.

However, explanation wasn't easy. Lots of jobs are hard to explain. One time I squawked when I crunched too hard on a bit of food, but I squawked louder when the dentist told me it would cost two hundred dollars to put that little tooth back in shape. A friend of mine works a couple of hours on that dentist's driveway with a clanking bulldozer and charges him only fifty bucks. Obviously neither of us understands dentistry. Another friend earns eighteen thousand dollars as an economics professor—with a total teaching load of three students a week. I don't understand economics, either.

A famous preacher once confessed that his sermons were made of toast, jam and coffee—nothing more complicated than that. And so it goes: the other person's job is a mystery.

Thus it was no great wonder that I had a hard time making myself clear to my neighbors down the road and up through the woods and over by Charlie's. Although it didn't look it, I was working while reading through a book, for instance, or staring out the window over a typewriter. Writers write, yes—as Larry Elliott had said. But they also read and take notes and drink coffee and answer letters. At least most of them do.

Peg and I tried to make it clear that all this activity—or the lack of it, when you sit and try to dream up the right phrase—can be just as important as when the words pour out in a torrent. Sometimes we felt we had made our point, but much of the time we probably didn't make sense. This we suspected when all we got for our explanations might be an "Oh. Well, that's nice. But what do you *do* when you're not doing anything?"

It helped a little to get that beanbake story in a magazine. The beanbake was a revival of the old custom of digging a hole in the ground, bigger than a bathtub, building a fire in it until you had about two feet of coals, and burying a great pot of beans in the coals—complete with home-cured salt pork, home-grown onions, and plenty of that Vermont maple syrup. You covered it with two feet of earth to hold the heat and let it simmer overnight.

Resurrected the following noon, the beans graced a picnic table made of a barn door on sawhorses. Other makeshift tables bore further results of Lincoln's quietly gorgeous home cook-ing—and the whole affair ended up in *Woman's Day* magazine. My neighbors were startled ("I didn't know you were writing all that down, Ron!"), flabbergasted ("You mean you had seconds on homemade ice cream and got paid for it, too?"), and not a little pleased ("Bigosh, they spelled my name right: E–n–o–l–a Pierce!").

To many of our friends, however, I am only doing that in-definable something—or nothing. Every few days, when I pick up the telephone, the conversation begins like this: "Since you don't work, Ron . . . "

Indeed, since I didn't work, I actually got sent to Washing-ton. Make of the statement what you will; you'll probably wonder what's so unusual about *that*. However, my trip was a two-day visit, not a political plum. And I went on behalf of those good Lincoln people. Indeed, I went on their money.

The occasion was the birthday of our postmaster. But it was hardly a celebration. Linny Bicknell had served long and well; now he had reached mandatory retirement age. He'd have to quit whether he wanted to or not.

Such a development, while scarcely unique, had a profound effect on our small village. The Post Office Department—as it was still called—had decided not to replace him. Instead, those few boxes and the stamp window in the front room of the house in the center would be retired, too. A treasured town gathering place would close forever. From now on four hun-dred people would no longer officially live in Lincoln, Ver-mont. As of June 1, 1968, there'd be no such address. At that time, the department notified each of us, we'd begin to reside somewhere along R.F.D. 1, Bristol.

Shaken, the townspeople called a hasty gathering at Burnham Hall in the center of the village. There were two hundred persons present—as many as you'd expect at the annual town meeting in March. Obviously Linny's birthday couldn't be postponed. Those terse cards marked *Official Business* had been regretfully distributed as one of his last magisterial acts. It looked as if the die was cast. But was it? "It don't say 'Positively,'" someone pointed out, "so maybe we still got a chance."

Well, maybe we did. After all, the place would be open for a few more weeks. Perhaps a delegate could go down to the postal headquarters in Washington and head off that closing date.

The idea took hold. Here, at least, was a way we could do something, instead of just letting the days go by like the ticking of a time bomb. "But who will go for us?" asked Marshall Hutchins, the meeting's impromptu moderator. "Who's got the time?"

This stumped them for a few minutes. It was sort of like a family of mice wondering who'd volunteer to go up and bell the cat. Then some character in the audience spoke up. "How about Ron Rood? He's not working."

Marshall looked questioningly in my direction. Ducking to avoid a direct hit, I bent over to tie my shoe. But Marshall's voice followed me right to the floor. "Well—how about it, Ron?"

"Uh," I began, but after a quick look at my friends my excuse died in my throat. Here was one positive way I could help them. Besides, it was going to work a hardship on me as much as anyone. I couldn't take manuscripts of questionable heft down to Linny's place and get them weighed any more. Nor could I trot down to Lincoln with insured, registered or certified mail. I'd have to take it the six miles to Bristol—unless I wanted to burden the rural carrier with the paperwork.

But the worst part of all was the closing of a hallowed institution. Half the life of Lincoln centered on the post office.

"You can do it," someone pep-talked from behind me. "I'd even go with you—if I had the time."

A few more voices were added, offering to hold my coat while I fought the good fight. Feeling like the rookie on the bench who is sent into the Big Game to sub for the injured quarterback, I found myself allowing as how I just might be able to go.

"It's worth a try," I admitted to these friends who had helped me so often, and who now looked to me for aid. "Besides," I said, justifying my decision in a burst of originality, "while there's life there's hope. The place doesn't close down for about a month yet."

Gleefully, the crowd accepted this as the way out. But they did more than sit back and cheer. Someone snatched off his hat, dropped a dollar into it, and sent it through the audience. By the time it had made the rounds it held enough for one round-trip ticket from Burlington to Washington.

Marshall handed me the hat with an exaggerated bow. "And here, Ron, is your plane fare. Meeting's adjourned."

Okay. Now I was the quarterback. But what would I do next?

The first thing, I decided, was to take Peg along. So, as my contribution to the effort, I bought her a ticket. Then we called Vermont's congressional delegation in Washington.

Senator George Aiken was furious. His home town of Putney wasn't much larger than Lincoln. "What the heck do they think they're doing?" he stormed. "Who the heck do they think they are? Why, they're cutting the heart out of a small town!"

Vermont's lone Congressman, Bob Stafford, was not in Washington at the moment, but Senator Winston Prouty echoed Aiken's sentiments: "What do those clowns know about rural Vermont down in this jungle, anyway?" he fumed.

Then he calmed down a bit. "My car will meet you at the airport," he promised. "Come to my office and we'll make you feel at home. Then we'll have someone for you to talk to."

Impressed and encouraged, Peg and I boarded the plane the following morning. Had our two senators not taken up the cudgel, we'd have felt lost and foolish. But with them riled up

48   RONALD ROOD

—well, the Post Office Department was about to hear from Lincoln again.

It heard from us, all right. With two senators running interference we got an audience with almost anybody we wanted. We followed the hierarchy right up through to the top—and there we were stopped cold. Not from lack of sympathy, however. It's just that our timing was bad.

Postmaster General Lawrence O'Brien was just stepping down from that top position, worse luck. The gentleman temporarily in command was merely minding the store, so to speak. After listening to our story he gave us the official explanation.

Tiny offices such as Linny's were markedly unprofitable, he pointed out. The postal service was reeling from financial setbacks as it was. Furthermore, to countermand the order that established Lincoln as a faceless rural route out of Bristol would practically take an Act of Congress.

Then he dropped the other shoe. "I can understand how you feel," he said, "because I've been through it myself. The town in Virginia where I make my home lost its post office two years ago. We yelled our heads off—but we survived."

Curses! We'd wanted argument—not agreement. The blow that is launched and lands on nothing may be like a boomerang. The one who launches it is apt to suffer as much as the intended target. *Now* what could we say?

He listened to us further. He agreed with everything we said, but the spark was gone. We couldn't confront him with an accusing "You don't know how it is," because he knew. At least partially.

So we returned empty-handed. But, in a way, we had the last word. Even if it didn't postpone the closing a second longer, we told our story to *Newsweek*. The magazine printed a picture of Linny Bicknell standing at the door of the expiring enterprise. Above his head was the sign POST OFFICE—LINCOLN, VT. And under the picture, along with a story about

"Since You Don't Work, Ron—"

the price of progress, was a quote attributed to its doughty postmaster, but as readily said by anybody in the town: "They're madder'n hornets!"

That was one little adventure I had because I didn't work, and I've had others, too—many of them. Actually, though, the feeling around Lincoln is not so much that I don't work as that I must have a whale of a lot of spare time.

People call me on the telephone and even come to see me "because I thought you needed a rest from all that writing you've been doing." I enjoy every visit, every phone call, and have learned a special trick to enable me to shift mental gears while keeping my motor running, so to speak. The trick was taught me by Dr. Benjamin Browne, late editor-in-chief of the American Baptist Publication Society.

"I'm interested in people," he told me, "and I've got to have them around. But they are human: they call me on the phone when *they* have time. Or they come to my door and politely wonder if I'm busy. Of course after they've said that, I'm no longer busy; I'm dying of curiosity."

And how did this busy man cope with interruptions? "Simple. You stop. Just like that. Right in mid-sentence, or even mid-word. Then when you get back to what you were doing, there's that dangling thought, just begging to be picked up again. If you wrap up a paragraph or sometimes even a sentence before dealing with the interruption, when you return to work you say to yourself, 'Fine. But what do I do now?' "

As with Ben Browne's, a vital part of my daily experience involves contact with people. Using Ben's trick I can answer a lady's hasty call for reassurance about a snake in her garden. Or I can be properly impressed when a bird-lover, brand new and wildly enthusiastic, appears at my door with a breathless yarn about two golden eagles and a turkey vulture at his feeder. I shake my head in unfeigned disbelief and admit, with complete candor, that I've never seen such a thing. Then, after scratching a couple of quick notes to preserve such gems for

RONALD ROOD

all time, I go back to my typewriter and pick up my waiting thought.

There's another reason for the impression that writing isn't work. If you've watched a fine performer like a good skater or a smooth dancer you know how effortless it all seems. There's nothing to it; that's obvious. In the same way, the finished product of an accomplished writer seems to have flowed easily from that gifted pen. "Why, I could have written that!" is the feeling we have all had at some time or other.

Hence, since writing is such a breeze, the writer must have it easy. Anybody can do it. Naturally, it helps not a bit to maintain that it just isn't that simple. After all, didn't Abraham Lincoln write the Gettysburg Address on an old envelope?

I have taken to carrying old envelopes, too. Not to produce another Gettysburg Address, of course, but just to have something for a note when the occasion offers. I jam such notes into my pocket and exhume them at bedtime. A friend of mine, who spends much of her writing career interviewing people, carries a newspaper instead of a pad. She says there's plenty of writing area in the blank spaces, and a simple newspaper puts the speakers at their ease. Neither a newspaper nor an envelope looks very professional—and there's that writer, not working again.

Yes, sermons—and stories, and scenarios for television—are made of coffee and toast. They're also made of remarks overheard on a bus, the shouts of children at play, the comments of the dentist or the bulldozer operator. We all hear them; a few people do something about them. Robert Frost was once asked how long he had worked on a certain poem. His reply: "All my life."

Priceless experiences are everywhere. Sometimes I lose them because I fail to jot them down fast enough. Sometimes I cannot use them because they're too personal and I'd injure those grand friends of mine. Add a daily pocketful of notes to the hours spent in reading, in tramping the woods, in lying motionless a hundred yards from a fox den with a telephoto camera, and it's small wonder that people have a hard time figuring out when I'm working.

Or even if I *am* working. Sometimes I'm a little hazy about that, myself.

RONALD ROOD

3. *How Many Bones in an Elephant?*

If you have used an encyclopedia very much, you're probably aware that it doesn't know everything. Even if it contained the last word on a subject, that last word might not be last for long. Encyclopedias are printed books, and books get old.

While the entry CAESAR, JULIUS may be in fine shape fifteen years after it was printed, you have the feeling that another, bravely labeled SPACE, EXPLORATION OF, may be out of date before it hits your shelf.

Your encyclopedia is a great help, but you wish to know more. So you do what people have been doing almost since the first printed word got out where people could read it: you send a question to whoever published it.

Newspapers and magazines sometimes respond to such letters in their pages. Many encyclopedias provide an answering service for their readers. Once you've become the owner of such an encyclopedia you are thus put in touch with its vast store of knowledge.

Let's say you've been chortling over Mark Twain's story of "The Celebrated Jumping Frog of Calaveras County," for instance. Then, as you sit back and think about what you've read, a question forms in your mind. Poor Daniel, the frog who'd been surreptitiously loaded down with so much buckshot that he couldn't move, must have been quite a jumper in his time. How far might he have vaulted if he'd been in better shape that day—ten feet? fifteen? twenty? More?

You look under FROG in your encyclopedia. There you find a description of the clammy-skinned critter, together with a number of its amphibian relatives. You learn there's a mink frog, a leopard frog, a cricket frog. There's even a picture of a bullfrog balanced on a lily pad in goggle-eyed glory. But nary a word is said about the distance it could cover in a single bound.

This was where I came in.

Or it could have been, up to a short time ago. For nearly twelve years I served as a researcher for half a dozen encyclopedias. Casting about, in those early days of writing, for something to keep the pot boiling between manuscripts, I had learned of encyclopedia readers' services. So I wrote to one of the large companies. Did they need a researcher in the field of natural history?

Well—yes and no. "What we need," they wrote back, "is someone who can search for information in many areas of science, not just natural history. If you'd be willing to consider a wide variety of questions, we'd be glad to talk with you further."

I allowed as how I'd be willing. We did talk further—and thus began one of the most fascinating decades any writer could expect. It was just what I wanted: the challenge of plunging into some learned publication—the *Journal of Psychophysiology*, say—and coming up with something most anybody could understand.

There seemed to be no limit to the questions that were asked. Children wondered about their pets, the world about them, their own bodies. So did their elders. The mother of a four-year-old, at a loss for an answer, wanted us to tell her daughter if clouds ever sleep. A home economics student wondered how a mother kangaroo could housebreak her baby. A college professor in New Mexico inquired about the famous musk ox herd maintained in Vermont by Dr. John Teal. A Korean woman who married an American soldier wondered what it meant when other G.I.'s told her spouse that he had lost all his marbles when he married her.

Some of the questions, like that one about the musk oxen, were easy to answer. There had been plenty of publicity about those arctic beasts that had been brought to a farm in Huntington, fifteen miles from my Vermont home. It was merely a matter of reading up about them and passing the information along to the professor in New Mexico. The cleanly kangaroo was an easy one, too: the mother performs necessary household chores until her baby is old enough for well-timed little visits to the outer world on its own.

Incidentally, the joey (the term for a kangaroolet) has a harder time cutting the apron strings than keeping its room tidy. It dives back into that pouch when danger threatens, even if the pouch has become several sizes too small and the youngster's panicky leap upsets the mother.

How Many Bones in an Elephant? 55

The Korean wife's question may have been sent to me because nobody else wanted to answer it. To understand why her husband's friends felt he lacked a few marbles, she needed two things herself: (1) a better command of American language, and (2) a sense of humor. I tried to help her gently on both counts, and just hoped she wouldn't take it all too personally.

Nearly every day for close to twelve years there'd be several letters in my mail. I half expected those postal inspectors back to update their reports any day. All told, I received more than ten thousand questions. Some could be answered from my own book collection. Others would send me scurrying to a college library at Burlington or Middlebury. Still others required a letter of my own to some authority or, in a rush, a hasty phone call for information.

Some of the hardest to answer were from young readers. Sometimes they weren't even readers yet, but with a marvelous sense of wonder that would set me to cudgeling my brains, or burrowing into my books. How would you answer that four-year-old who wondered if clouds ever went to sleep, for instance? As I recall, I told the little girl who asked about the clouds that things got sleepy when they got tired, and since clouds just drifted they never got tired.

Here are a few more sample questions:

"My father and I were talking about what we would have for breakfast and I wondered what the Pilgrims had for breakfast. My father and I both didn't know. Do you?"

"I asked my mother why I should eat my spinach and she said I should know. I looked in my books and couldn't find out why. Can you tell me?"

"Our son, age five, has requested an answer to this question at least once a day for the past month: 'How can our small eyes see such big things?'"

"My teacher asked me to write to you to see if you could answer us a question? The question is 'If gravity pulls down, why do we grow up?'"

This one should gladden the hearts of television sponsors everywhere. "Why does my one-year-old son stop whatever he is doing and concentrate on the commercial? Television commercials may not be loud but rather soft and boring, but even if the baby happens to be in another room he will come to watch the commercial and then return to his play."

While the sponsor may nod in satisfaction with such a letter, I can just hear the weary viewers: "Aha! I told you so!"

The curiosity of children goes far beyond television or their own physical beings, of course. Here are a few sample questions on the world about us:

"Does a cat have nine lives? Ours just died and it was the first time. Why is this?"

"I am ten years old. I asked my daddy what trees are made of and he said 'wood.' I asked him what wood is made of and he said I better ask you."

"Does a frog bump his bottom when he jumps?"

"I am twelve years old. This morning I got to wondering about fire bugs. Is there a bug that starts fires? I want to know how one starts a fire and what they look like and if there is any in Idaho. We looked in the books and can't find it there."

"Do dogs, cats, and cows have baby teeth like humans do? I am ten years old and in the fifth grade."

"I was in the backwoods of Oregon and I heard a scream. My father said it was the scream of the cougar. If not, what was it?"

And what were the answers to these questions? As I said, the curiosity of children can pose a problem. However, we tried to keep the answers simple, knowing that sometimes the more you explain the worse the problem may get. Small eyes can see huge things, I told that youngster, in the same way that you can see the whole world when you peek through a little hole. My suggestion was that he try looking through the cardboard tube from a roll of toilet paper. I don't know if it worked or not, but I hoped it'd help. At least it would give him something to do.

How Many Bones in an Elephant?

In providing the answers to questions, we were obligated only to the extent that such information could be found in print. Original research—such as getting a frog and finding out what bumps when it jumps—was beyond our responsibility.

However, there were occasional requests that were too fascinating to leave alone. The frog question was such a case. Peg and I both happen to be interested in water creatures, so we took a number of flash photos of jumping frogs. We learned that those gangly-legged critters land in all sorts of ways—front feet first, hind feet first, belly-whackers, nose dives. Apparently grace is not one of the strong points of your average frog.

This brings up the question posed earlier in this chapter. Assuming an auspicious take-off, just how far can a frog travel before it comes to earth again—no matter how undignified the landing?

To find the answer, we wrote to the Calaveras County Frog Jumping Contest in California. That's right, there is such an event. We learned that, back in 1954, to the cheers of the frenzied crowd, a superfrog named Lucky put a whopping 16

RONALD ROOD

feet 10 inches of California air between hop and flop. Which —stories being what they are—would doubtless have been duck soup to Mark Twain's Daniel if he hadn't been half shot at the time.

I answered a couple of other questions with original research as well. They happened to arrive in our mail just before we were to take a youth group for a trip to New York City.

The first question came from a reader who wondered what would happen to an ant if it tumbled off a skyscraper. "If it fell off the Empire State Building," she asked, "would it die or float down?"

Having seen insects fall from tables with no apparent damage, I figured the same would be true in the case of a tall building. However, since I was going to visit New York, why not try it to see what would happen? Perhaps I could watch the first ten feet, anyway.

Thus, when we arrived at the Empire State's observation platform high above the street, I told the group to help me see what happened. Flicking a few ant-sized pieces of dust into the air, we began our experiment.

But we never finished it. Carried by the heated air rising from the streets below, the "ants" actually soared out of sight above us. And so, although the reader's question may have been tongue-in-cheek, it received the straight-faced answer as solemnly attested by eleven pairs of eyes: the ant wouldn't fall at all. Not there, at least. And, air resistance being what it is, it'd probably settle as lightly as a feather when it did land.

The other question that sent me off on an exploration in New York City involved a college student's interest in anatomy. "How many bones," he asked, "are there in an elephant?"

Since our group was scheduled for a visit to the American Museum of Natural History, I toted that question along in my mind. Then, while the youngsters wandered fascinated through those halls, I sought out what I hoped would give me the answer.

At last I found what I wanted: the mortal remains of that

How Many Bones in an Elephant?

most portentous of ponderous pachyderms—P. T. Barnum's
Jumbo. Even as a skeleton, the great beast was impressive. He
stood nearly eleven feet high at the shoulder—one foot higher
than a basketball hoop. His skull looked as big as a bathtub,
and his ribs looked like the timbers of a ship. No task to count
those huge bones, I figured.

I began counting. The main body was easy, but the head
and tail were so high in the air that I kept losing my place.
Finally I prevailed on a sympathetic attendant—who doubtless
chalked up my antics as a fringe benefit of his job—to provide
me with a stepladder.

For the next half-hour I ascended and descended, like a
sculptor sizing up a block of granite before striking the first
blow. Some mammals have a little bone, called the hyoid, at
the base of the tongue; was Jumbo so blessed? Even though
his trunk was all muscle and cartilage—and, hence, not a part
of the skeleton—were there any bones at its base? And how
about that little segment at the end of his tail—was it one bone
or two?

At last I arrived at a conclusion. Folding the ladder, I returned it to the attendant. Then I joined the youngsters in the
museum cafeteria. "Well?" inquired Peg. "How many?"

"Two hundred eight. I think."

"You *think*? After an hour? What's the matter—wouldn't
he stand still?"

I explained the problem, drank my coffee, piled the kids
into the car, drove home—and wrote a letter to the museum.
They informed me that the number may vary with the individual, but it's usually about two hundred sixteen. I'd missed
about half a dozen bones somewhere.

So much for original research.

Incidentally, in case you wonder what such a creature
would eat, you're as curious as a lady in Des Moines. In answer
to her request, I sent a letter to the National Zoo in Washington. They informed me that an elephant in good appetite
would consume two meals a day. Its rations would total two

bales of hay per day, plus about three gallons of crushed oats or bran, ten loaves of bread ("more or less, depending on the elephant"), with an occasional snack of an armload of fruit or vegetables.

Elephants are impressive, yes. So are other critters—for instance, ice worms and hoop snakes, and fur-bearing trout. And did you know that an alligator swallows a log before it hibernates? Or that there really is such a creature as a mermaid?

Encyclopedia readers, looking through their books for the identity of such intriguing individuals, often draw a blank. Then, shortly, it's up to the research service to start hunting. The interesting thing about these and many other myths, I discovered, is that they bear at least a grain of truth.

Consider the mythical hoop snake, for instance. Supposedly it takes its tail in its mouth and rolls downhill. Knowing how people often reach for a stick when they see a snake, and how one of these creatures may bite at its own body when wounded, it's not hard to put two and two together—and get five or six, or whatever the occasion demands.

Ice worms, naturally, are worms that live in glacial ice. Supposedly they feed and grow fat on the frozen crystals. Although such a critter has never been captured, it's very much alive in people's imagination. I have photographed the Vermont version of the ice worm on the glittering surface of the swamp near our house in the dead of winter. Crawling along in the bright winter sunshine there may be scores of caterpillars. The sun warms the grass clumps where they are resting, causing them to waken from their winter sleep. Uncurling, they begin to walk about—and there are your ice worms.

There are even fur-bearing trout, too—of a sort. The original fish doubtless got away before the astonished viewer could haul it out of the water, but today its cousins still swim in Lake Memphremagog in northern Vermont. Supposedly the fur is to keep the fish warm in these deep waters along the Canadian border. More likely, the fuzzy coating is the growth of a fungus that often attacks members of the trout and salmon family. However, a story should never lose in the telling, so fur-bearing trout they are.

That question about the alligator swallowing a log came from a reader in Louisiana. He wondered if the encyclopedia could shed any light on why the reptile does such a thing before retiring during unfriendly weather. No question as to *whether* it gulps down a log: just the hope that we'd tell him *why*.

Once again, there's a nugget of truth in the story. In advance of a winter snooze, many animals take apparently nonsensical foods. They're sometimes called "stuffing foods." Our Vermont black bear dines on such dainties as twigs, sticks and dry leaves. The innards of slumbering chipmunks, woodchucks, skunks and raccoons have been found to contain bits of grass, dried weeds and gravel. These morsels probably serve to keep the digestive tract open. In addition, any such scratchy surface may stimulate the intestines enough so they'll be ready for a more prosaic meal in the spring. After all, even you and I need roughage in our diet. Or, to be more delicate, bulk.

The capacious maw and stretchy gullet of an alligator may accommodate astonishing mouthfuls. For all their teeth, alligators are not given to much chewing: one gulp and it's down. And, I suspect, sizable twigs and other condiments found in the stuffing food of a drowsy alligator may grow into respectable logs by the time the story is told at third—or fourth—hand.

The mermaid, I learned, is known as the manatee, or sea cow. Shaped somewhat like a person on top, it has flipper arms and a flat, paddle-like tail. Its breasts are in the appropriate place from a human viewpoint, and it often drifts upright in the water while it suckles its young.

To a sailor who'd been at sea too long, such a creature must have appeared like a marine madonna. However, closer acquaintance would probably dampen his ardor. His lady love might weigh nearly half a ton. She'd have bleary eyes, skin like a football, and a whiskery kiss that would be like snuggling up to a broom.

RONALD ROOD

Nevertheless, a good myth can easily triumph over reality. Thus the sea cows are favored with the scientific name Sirenia: the alluring ladies of the sea.

It was an education in itself, receiving all those letters. Sometimes you had to read between the lines, or restate the question in your own mind before you could answer it. "We have some small river clams that are in danger of extinction—" got an airmail reply; I figured the clams had been captured by vacationers, perhaps, and now were perishing because nobody knew what to do next. A Michigan reader's request for "a list of diseases of Michigan foresters" needed to lose a couple of letters from that last word before I could give much of an answer.

I was tickled by the question sent to me by a sixth-grader. He wanted us to "Please send the origin and history of the Jersey Cow and pitchers if possible." The misspelling in another letter was, in some way, better than it might have been if more correctly presented: "I would like to know how the snow crystals form their buetyful shapes."

And, if you've ever looked at snowflakes through a microscope you may agree that they are indeed "buetyful." Especially if you draw each syllable out as you say the word. There's hardly a better way to express it.

Because a lady in Ohio wanted to know, I learned how a fly lands on a ceiling. Apparently it flies close enough to graze the surface. Then it puts its front two legs up, grabs hold, and ends up facing in the opposite direction. I learned that a honeybee may make a beeline of a mile between flower and hive; that the red cells in our bloodstream may live only thirty days; that a certain female guppy in a fish tank in New Jersey received all the attention from the males, even though there were other females present ("I ask my husband why he thinks this is so, and all he does is smile").

There were students who wondered how to set up an exhibit at a science fair, farmers who asked about their livestock, and a fisherman who had heard that August was a poor month for fishing because that was when the fish lost all their teeth. A hotel manager wondered if the bats in the upstairs rooms would disappear in winter (yes, they would). And a mayor sent a rush request in hopes we could help him get rid of the pigeons on the front of city hall (we sympathized with him, gave him several suggestions—and wished him good luck).

One man had read that the Indians used to catch fish by "tickling"—feeling carefully beneath the overhanging bank of a stream to grab a fish resting in the shadows. He wanted to know just how it was done—"and what happens if you tickle a snapping turtle?" A teenager wondered if it was true that goats gave homogenized milk (yes, it's true), while a sergeant in an air base in Texas wondered if ants ever got hooked on tobacco—he had seen them lugging away the filter tips of discarded cigarettes. A Pennsylvania high school junior had heard about irradiated or "hot" male insects being used somehow in pest control and wondered if we'd give her the lurid details.

I checked on this last item with the U.S. Department of Agriculture and found that the story was indeed true. Treated with radioactive materials, the males of certain insects become sterile. However, they still have the power to mate. Foisted off

RONALD ROOD

by the millions on an unsuspecting native population, these supermales pair up with the local ladies and produce—nothing.

The cigarette-loving ants, by the way, act as they do because of sweeteners in the tobacco. Concentrated in the discarded filter tips, the sweeteners lie there, perfuming the countryside. The ants, poking about on foraging expeditions, find them irresistible.

Prodded by the curiosity of our correspondents, I snooped into every corner of our world. Did somebody wonder about deep-sea monsters? I'd give a full report—as soon as I found out myself. Was it true that there were spiders in the eternal snows of lofty mountains? Yes; they'd been carried there by updrafts and might remain there frozen forever.

There were even people who wished for the moon—almost literally. They wanted us to do a term paper or college thesis, complete with footnotes and a bibliography. After my initial shock at the first few such requests, I worked out a stratagem that would maintain what I figured was my own code of ethics. Finding a source of material on the subject, I'd pass the information along to the reader, plus a reading list for him to pursue on his own.

"In this way," I told Peg, "I'm giving the student the help he needs, but I'm not taking his college course for him."

Peg agreed. "Good idea. Besides—what if you flunked?"

Such letters arrived two or three a day in late winter and early spring. Apparently students saw the moment of truth approaching. I always tried to let them down easy. After all, I was there once, myself.

One big area where people looked for help was in the things that happen just because we're all so mortal and human. In hot water at home or on the job, or perhaps unlucky in romance, we all are grateful for someone to listen to our troubles. Frequently the best solution lies right at hand, but when we're wrought up and worried it's hard to see. Hence, we turn to someone else: our pastor, perhaps, or a trusted friend. While strictly personal problems weren't my province, I could help

How Many Bones in an Elephant?   65

with those involving the living world or some physical situation. I answered nearly a thousand such questions.

Even today as I write this, some fifteen years after I gave up my work for the research service, I still may think about some of the woes that beset those readers. I wonder how they got out of their difficulties and whether time did indeed turn out to be the great healer. I feel that such must have been the case, for instance, with the army corporal, newly sent overseas to a Pacific outpost, whose pain of homesickness was exquisitely wrapped in his short but eloquent plea: "What causes loneliness?"

Time must have come to the rescue, too, of the many parents who wrote for assistance in explaining the Facts of Life to their children. It must have healed the anguish of the small boy who lost his parakeet and wrote to ask us why. Doubtless time also played a hand in solving the problem of a girl whose father said she could not have a kitten "although my mother and my grandmother say it is all right." I've often wondered how *that* one came out.

All good things, the proverb claims, come to those who wait. I just hoped this would be the case for a lad who found himself with this problem:

"I would like for you to send me some psychology on how to get your dad to get you a scooter when it only costs $60 and I loned him $70. Its a good used scooter starts every time, has good brakes and it is safe. Send me three ways."

Or take the dilemma of this youngster, whose parents helpfully stated his case for him:

"Our 6 yr old son would like to know why he is so very good in school and so very nasty and sassy to Mom & Dad."

An eight-year-old wondered "what is wrong with not eating vejtables," while a girl who'd reached the limits of patience in trying to train her dog sputtered, "Why don't animals talk our language anyway?"

One boy in San Diego sent me into far more research than he probably planned when he asked the simple but searching question, "What kind of a person would man be if he had the ability to use all of his brain, and exactly what would he be capable of doing?"

I sent him the figure, variously quoted from Einstein and others, indicating that many of us normal human beings may use as little as one percent of our mental capacity. Then I listed a few exercises—such as the making of shopping lists, the use of telephone directories, the itemizing for grocery check-out totals—which might not be committed to figures on paper if we were more agile upstairs. Wars, famine, pestilence and taxes might become perils of the past. Then rather lamely, as I'm a one-percenter myself, I suggested that a full answer would be hard to obtain—precisely because we don't use all of our brains and hence cannot know what would happen.

The boy's question got me to thinking, however. One percent of our brains—or even five or ten—what a waste of the rest! What, indeed, could we do if we used all our mental and physical powers?

So I pried into my old college textbooks and haunted the library. I studied those technical journals with the impossible titles, hoping to find what we'd be like if we ran at anywhere near the efficiency we expect from most other machines.

The answer never revealed itself, as far as I could discover. Perhaps this was because nobody was qualified to present it. Of course, I probably wouldn't have recognized it, anyway. However, I did have the joy of rediscovering the old biblical truth in modern jawbreaking journalese—that we are, indeed, fearfully and wonderfully made.

A couple of examples. Take those apparently simple units of which you and I are built. Each of our several trillions of cells is a beehive of activity. It constantly undergoes all the basic body activities: growth, repair, and respiration, to name just three. In the process each single cell, even when it's apparently resting, may be performing two hundred tiny chemical reactions at once—and some scientists think this figure is ridiculously low.

To supply energy for such a task, in a lifetime the heart must pump enough blood to float a battleship. This blood races through a maze of vessels whose combined length would reach a quarter of the way to the moon. To supply oxygen to that blood, each breath we take filters into lung sacs whose total surface area may equal that of a tennis court. And so on, through all the systems of the body.

(I told about some of this fantastic activity to a high school class where I was invited to give a talk. Many of the students, so jaded by superlatives in advertising and the news, were scarcely impressed. The eyes of one girl, however, got wider by the minute. And, when I paused in my description of the bustling community that is the human body, she seized her chance. "Good grief!" she blurted. "How can we sleep?")

As a spin-off in connection with my interest in what makes us go, I found myself with several pounds of notes. They've helped in a variety of magazine articles and books, including these few words in this one. And I still wonder what you and I could do if we were to use all our powers. Doubtless I'll never find the answer to my young friend's request. But it's been fun trying.

A few more questions in the field of human endeavor:

"I am doing a study of W. C. Fields. Please tell me all the funny things that happened in his life."

"What would one do if he was lost in the Okefenokee Swamp? Please rush reply, as I need it immediately."

The subject of marriage always produces its share of perplexities. A young New Hampshire man, perhaps casting around for a way out, wondered how he would know when he could afford to get married. A college co-ed, viewing marriage from another angle, wondered if we'd give her "a few examples of famous women in history or literature who continued to love their husband after he had done something wrong." Luckily she asked for just a sampling of the subject, or my answer would have had to be a long one.

Married couples occasionally used the research service as a

sounding board for their differences. One husband had no question to ask, but merely favored us with the statement that if a man felt he had won an argument with a woman, the argument wasn't over yet. A Connecticut wife felt she'd won her particular point, but wanted us to clinch it for her. "We have wild morning glory on our lawn," she wrote, "and my husband thinks the lawn will kill the morning glory out. I don't think so. I think the morning glory will kill everything else out. Who is right?"

And then came the little remark that told us just who obviously *was* right. "P.S.," it said. "Please send me the names of several good weed killers."

A foretaste of today's marriage-that-isn't came out of a high school science fair on Long Island, although I'm not sure that's what the young lady had in mind. She wanted information " . . . because I'm participating in a science demonstration. I am planning on a physical project about man's future living underwater with a classmate."

People are always interested in the human side of animals. This has long been a fascinating subject to me, too. I looked forward to receiving such letters. One farm wife asked if a chicken goes through as much pain laying an egg as a woman does having a baby. A Kentucky lad wondered if horses dream. Another youngster asked the very question that perplexed me when I was growing up on our small farm in Connecticut. "What do cows think about," he wondered, "when they're hitched in the stanchion all night?"

Incidentally, there is indeed such a thing as boredom in animals. A blooded race horse may have a "mascot"—a pigeon, perhaps, or a chicken, or a little dog—that accompanies it on its journeys and helps while away the long hours in the stable. Sometimes, apparently because of nothing better to do, a horse will get to chewing on the wood of a door or window, often inhaling in great, gusty sighs as it chews. The habit is known as "cribbing," and is almost impossible to break.

Dairy bulls are sometimes given a sturdy barrel or a big

chunk of wood to push around while in the exercise pen. Such animals are apt to be better tempered than bulls which have nothing to do, and therefore are spoiling for a fight. Dogs are less apt to bark and howl if a radio is playing when the family is away. Almost any puppy, kitten or other young animal will grow to a more normal adulthood if it has some kind of playmate during those formative months.

The "thoughts" of a cow in its stanchion, according to an animal behaviorist to whom I addressed that reader's question, are probably half-formed reactions to sights and sounds of the barn: a mouse in the manger, the rattling of a window, the steady rhythm of other cows chewing the cud. "It is really hard to estimate what occupies the bovine attention," he wrote. Then he added an extra little fillip: "Besides, we humans do not even understand our own thoughts half the time."

On the subject of animals and their mental powers, one reader wondered "if animals other than humans are aware of being pregnant? If they do, how do they react?"

For an answer to this one, I was able to draw on my own observations. Peg and I have seen female rabbits pull hair from their bodies to line the nest as the time of birth approaches. I also remembered searching through the bushes down by the pasture brook when Daisy was due to have her calf: invariably I'd find her and her offspring in a little glen surrounded by the densest, meanest patch of briars she could find. Some pregnant wild female mammals may turn on their mates and thrash them within an inch of their lives before the astonished males make their escape. A mother squirrel may carry out her version of re-arranging the furniture by building two or three nests until she hits on one that apparently suits her.

Such antics do not necessarily mean an actual awareness of the impending blessed event. Nevertheless, they are dramatic changes in behavior even if the animal herself couldn't explain why she did them. Or so it would seem. But then, who can psychoanalyze a squirrel?

We were also called upon by people who wanted to assist

those female animals in their maternal duties. Because we did hear from youngsters so often, almost in self-defense we prepared some mimeographed notes on general animal care. Then, when a suitable question arrived, I'd take the mimeo sheet, jot a few notes of my own on it, and send it off to the reader. This was a great timesaver. Besides, if you've got an Easter chick clamoring to be fed and you're waiting to see if the know-how is in today's mail, a quick answer may mean the difference between life and death for the helpless creature.

Animals, however, are individuals. So are the people who care for them. Thus that prepared sheet did not always answer the question. Here are a few examples of ones that needed a letter, too.

I was able to call on personal experience in my reply to a boy who wondered how to set himself up in the business of worm-farming. He wanted to know how many acres were in the average worm farm, so I figured it out. The answer: about one ten-thousandth of an acre, or the size of a washtub. At least that was the size of the worm farm I'd had as a youngster.

Like so many farmers, I found the enterprise rich in experience but not in money. My problem was that there were not enough customers. The worms proliferated in apparent high spirits, but the fishermen didn't follow suit. To boost my chances I considered such economic wizardry as withholding the current crop and thereby creating a scarcity. Such a tactic would work, I figured. Except for one detail: nobody would know the difference. So after a bad fiscal year with the near-term prospects looking dark, I decided to flood the market.

Overturning that washtub in a corner of Mother's flower garden on a rainy day, I watched my wriggling charges burrow down into the soil and disappear into the largest worm farm most of them had ever known. From that time on, the fishermen would have to take their business elsewhere. They had had their chance.

I explained the hazards of worm-farming in my answer to the young reader. I told him that with proper care his worm farm would grow by leaps and bounds—at least, figuratively. The worms would be willing, I told him, but the fishermen might fail. Here was one enterprise where grassroots support, so to speak, would not be enough.

There were other farming questions, too, on more prosaic subjects. People were interested in horses, in cattle, in what sheep would thrive best in Nova Scotia, and would a hen lay eggs if there was no rooster around. One young couple wanted us to provide "all the information needed to make a success in farming." A member of a high school F.F.A. (Future Farmers of America) chapter started a letter, crossed out the first paragraph, and finished with this hymn to the scope of our research:

"In place of farm buildings, please send me the different breeds of cattle. If this is not possible, please send pictures."

An unanswerable question? Not really—unless you took his first sentence literally. If you read between the lines a bit, you'd realize what he meant. Besides, supposedly there is no such thing as an unanswerable question. One reader came close, though, when he wished to have us give him "some information on the ethics of horse trading." As a Yankee who had grown up on a farm where I'd seen horse traders at work, I was tempted to give him a simple three-word reply: "There ain't any."

There may be an answer to every question, but a geologist friend of mine wasn't so sure. Or at least he wasn't sure he wanted to answer the questions that came to him.

My friend was a researcher for a number of organizations. One group received a trio of questions and sent them along to him. The requests came from a man in Brooklyn. His first concerned the ocean around New York City. What were the times of high and low tide, he wished to know, for the days of the last half of February?

Such information is readily available: fishermen need to know, as do ships' masters and tugboat captains. Tides may be merely a rise and fall of the waterline when you're swimming at the beach, but they can hamper or help the efforts of a ship to come into a harbor. The current of a running tide may turn a placid inlet into a foaming river as thousands of tons of water run out to sea. Then the river reverses itself and the water comes roaring back in response to the gravitational pull of the moon.

My friend checked the tide tables and sent the information to the questioner. In a couple of weeks a second request arrived. This one was more specific. What would be the speed and direction of the tide in the channel between Staten Island and the lower tip of Manhattan at 10 P.M. on a certain evening?

A close study of the appropriate tide schedules produced the answer. This information was also sent to the client. He replied with thanks—and said he wished to ask one more question. Supposing an object weighing 160 pounds was released at the surface. How far would it drift before it came to rest on the bottom?

How Many Bones in an Elephant? 73

The whole affair sounded a little ominous. Taken aback, my friend replied by saying he required more information in order to answer the question. What was the nature of the object to be dropped, anyway?

"A big anchor," was the cheerful reply. "Just in case I happened to be out there in a yacht and had to stay for the night. How much anchor chain would I need?"

Suspicions unfounded. But it was almost a whodunit, at any rate.

All those questions, appearing unheralded in the mailbox at the end of my bridge, made for a fascinating twelve years. I'd probably still be answering them, too, if luck hadn't favored my free-lance efforts. But it was hard to be steeped in writing my own books here in Vermont and have to drop everything because someone in Virginia, say, needed sudden action. So I reluctantly decided that the research service would have to get along without me. And not only the research service: all those wonderful readers, too. Someone else is doubtless answering their questions. As I think of it, I feel just a little touch of envy.

Looking back over these last few pages, I realize that I left out the replies to many of the questions. Every one of the queries was answered at the time, however; and if you're interested, someone at the encyclopedias will mail you each answer again. If your encyclopedia provides a readers' research service, that is.

Otherwise—or unless your question is one of the others in the next chapter—you may have to drop anchors, worry about the mentality of cows, and contemplate the mortal remains of elephants all on your own.

4. *A Little Curiosity*

Did you know that the skunk cabbage can build its own greenhouse? Or that you can burn an amoeba, and boil it, and jump on it—but it goes right on living? Or that dormant grubs and bugs, hiding from the cold in their hollow trees, are half pickled all winter?

Well, it can. It does. And they are.

These and other tidbits come to light when you're on the receiving end of all those encyclopedia questions. There's nothing like a little curiosity to bring them out into the open. I cannot resist sharing a few more of them with you.

First, about the skunk cabbage and its cohorts in the opening paragraph. That aromatic plant, in case you're not well acquainted with it, has leaves that are large and green and thick, like a cabbage. Their odor is decidedly skunky. Living in marshy places, the plant sends up a red and yellow hooded blossom, something like a jack-in-the-pulpit, while frost is still in the ground. It may make its way up through as much as a foot of frozen soil.

To melt the ice, the deeply buried root converts some of its stored starch to sugar. The chemical change produces heat, sometimes raising the temperature to that of the human body. The plant thaws its way upward. It pokes its smelly red and yellow blossom out for the attentions of newly emerged carrion flies and beetles. Thus the skunk cabbage flower may be half through its career before other plants have even begun to grow.

The never-say-die amoeba? This blob of living jelly outlasts your best efforts to do it in because of its peculiar way of reproduction. When ready to give birth, so to speak, it undergoes a complex internal alteration. Then it splits in two. Each new fragment contains about half the original creature. You can easily snuff out one portion, but its mate continues undisturbed somewhere else.

Since each amoeba is really one-half of its parent, a quarter of its grandparent, and so on, the seemingly defenseless bit of protoplasm is practically immortal. So are similar beings that

RONALD ROOD

multiply by dividing: other protozoans, simple algae, and many bacteria.

Those slumbering insects and their apparently pixilated state are readily explained. With the onset of cold weather, the insect's body fluids begin to change. Some of them are chemically reshuffled to substances akin to the alcohol and ethylene glycol you put in your car radiator. Thus, on the bitterest night, the chilly insect may be dead to the world, but at least it will not turn into an icicle.

So antifreeze is scarcely new. Nor, for that matter, are plenty of our other cherished inventions. Spurred by those readers with their questions, I learned we'd been living in the jet age since long before the Wright brothers, for instance: the ancestors of the squid and octopus squirted their way through the primal seas millions of years before the first dinosaur appeared. Electric eels and torpedo rays generated electricity eons before Franklin flew his kite. Snorkels are standard equipment on some turtles. The diving spider has long been making an underwater apartment and carrying life-giving air down to it. We humans are still working on *that* one.

Gas warfare? Any stink bug can teach you about it. So can the bombardier beetle, with its rear-mounted popgun. So, too, can many female moths, in a way. Their come-hither scent may entice a male more than a mile distant when the wind is right.

Hypodermic needles? Get an instant education from a hornet.

Mind control? Watch the tarantula "hawk" as the huge wasp apparently paralyzes its spidery victim through sheer terror—and then ensures its victory by a well-placed sting that deprives the tarantula of motion forever.

The perfect society? Witness a well-ordered anthill. Its thousands live together with nary a quarrel among themselves. This laboring class is made of females whose reproductive organs are shriveled or have never developed. Such a harmonious state of affairs led my questioner to an interesting point: "If socialism is like a big, happy ant mound, why do the ants sterilize all their workers?"

Some questions came up again and again:

Q. Why do leaves turn color in the fall?

A. Actually, the color is there all the time. It is just that it's masked by the overwhelming quantity of green chlorophyll produced fresh daily for food production. When the leaf tapers off its normal activities in late summer, the green color fades, leaving the reds and yellows.

Q. How can those woolly-bear caterpillars forecast what kind of winter we'll have?

A. The art of caterpillar-reading can scarcely be committed to paper, but it concerns the two black ends of this common species, plus its rust-colored center section. The forward portion is believed to represent the first part of winter: the more extensive it is, the more severe the season's beginning. The wider the central brown band, the longer the winter will last. The nether end, naturally, finishes things off.

The next time you discover one of these close-cropped little critters in a heap of leaves or running along a sidewalk, try your own weather predictions. But don't expect any further co-operation from *Isia isabella*. As soon as the chill begins in earnest, the little weather prophet curls up and sleeps the rest of the winter.

Q. Is there any truth to the story of Groundhog Day?

A. Interestingly, yes. The groundhog, or woodchuck, is often a fitful sleeper. It may awake from dormancy several times during the winter. One of these dates may well be on February 2—and there's your groundhog, right on time.

Don't laugh too hard at the part where the animal retreats if it sees its shadow, either. Weather often runs in cycles. A sunny period alternates with a cloudy one, and vice versa. Thus, while *Marmota monax* may not actually give a hoot about its shadow, a fair day is apt to be followed by less salubrious weather. Hence the animal had better not stay out long, according to the laws of chance: things are bound to change.

RONALD ROOD

On the other hand, a gray day could well precede a sunny period. A groundhog that stuck it out might thus find better times ahead.

One weather-related topic that kept arising even in those days before high fuel prices was that of winter heating. Studies in forestry and my early days of camping had whetted my interest, so a number of questions came to me. Here are a few of them:

Q. What is the best wood for heating?

A. Dry wood. Hard wood. Wood that keeps a fire for a long time. Wood that throws few, if any, sparks—especially if you've got an open fireplace or Franklin stove. Generally, the denser the wood the better for heating. Maple, oak, beech and apple make good, long-burning fires. Pine and spruce ignite easily, but they burn out quickly. Besides, they throw sparks on the rug.

Q. Is it cheaper to heat with wood than with coal, oil, gas or electricity?

A. That all depends. What kind of wood is it? Has it been cut and seasoned for at least several months? Did you cut it yourself? If not, how much did you pay for it? What about possible safety problems if there are small children?

The U.S. Bureau of Home Economics says that as much as half the annual heating cost may be saved by using wood—even more on a cut-it-yourself basis. But it's not all money in the bank. There are a few trade-offs to consider.

If you burn wood, chances are you heat only a portion of the house. Then there's the ashes and soot, plus the burned spot in the carpet. There is the sweaty task of cutting, loading, stacking and carrying this "fuel that warms you twice," as it has been called.

There is also a little problem of supply. It may take up to ten acres of trees to meet the needs of a family on a continuing basis. That's only sixty-four families per square mile—more or less, depending on growth and management of the forest.

All considered, therefore, there'll probably be no shortage

A Little Curiosity

79

of unromantic souls who'll continue to meet their heating desires by pushing up the thermostat. And paying the bills.

Q. How big is a cord of wood, anyway?

A. A cord of wood was originally the amount a man could cut and stack in a working day. It was a pile 4 feet high, 4 feet wide and 8 feet long.

Now, with the current demand for wood, all kinds of quantities show up. In Vermont, for instance, you can buy a "rick" (half a cord) a "run" (a third of a cord) or, often, merely a "truckload"—the measurement of which may be anybody's guess.

Q. I'm trying to save fuel by turning down the thermostat at night. My friends say the furnace has to work harder in the morning to bring the house back to heat again and I lose all I've saved. Do I really lose, or do I gain?

A. You gain. Depending on your location and the difference between outdoor and indoor temperatures, you may save from 6 to 25 percent of your fuel bill by turning the heat down at night, according to government reports.

RONALD ROOD

Q. Can I make a living on a couple of acres and a garden?

A. Not if that's all you have. A few acres and independence —it's an old and cherished dream. However, even if you cut your own wood and grow your own groceries and clothing material, you've got to be an expert to start with. Thousands of worn-out farms sold for taxes and broken up for building lots show that it's not an easy job.

Besides, unless you're practically Dan'l Boone the Third, you'll still appreciate all your helpful neighbors, seen and unseen. These include the people that generate your electricity, make the paraffin for your candles, or refine the kerosene for your lamps. They'll be there, maintaining the road, giving you a lift to town, supplying the well-bred sheep you use to grow your own wool—and protecting your little spread from other less enterprising neighbors all over the world who might try to take it for themselves.

Q. In living off the land, should I stay clear of using certain animals as food? Are there any animals poisonous to eat?

A. Apparently not, as far as actual healthy flesh is concerned. Even the venom of a deadly snake is contained in special glands that are quite distinct from the rest of the animal. Rattlesnake meat, in fact, has long been considered a prime delicacy.

An animal that has died of unknown causes may be another matter. If it expired from poisoning, say, some of the poison may have entered the bloodstream. It may be found throughout the body. Certain organs, such as the liver and kidneys, may also contain toxic substances and should be avoided.

Q. Suppose I have been bitten by a rattlesnake. Will sucking venom from the bite be injurious if I have cavities in my teeth?

A. There would be little danger. All the suction would tend to draw everything into the mouth cavity rather than force it into the teeth and tissues. The same would be true of other injuries: cold-sores, chapped lips, etc.

Incidentally, snake venom is of a protein nature. If some is swallowed, it'll merely be digested.

Q. My friend says the human mouth is scarcely a model of cleanliness and that even a dog's mouth may be cleaner. She says it is all right to allow a dog to lick a baby's hands and face, etc. What do you say?

A. She is at least partially right. Our mouths are veritable gardens of bacteria, yeasts, molds and, often, small protozoans.

As for comparison with the mouth of a dog, it depends on the dog. Somebody's forgotten pooch may scrounge up an interesting collection from a local garbage pail, it is true. Nevertheless, as long as there are babies and there are dogs, each will kiss and love the other. The objection to the practice is probably more aesthetic than biological—especially when you consider all the other things that babies put in their mouths.

Q. Is it true that cows, etc., have no front teeth above?

A. Yes. This characteristic is shared by most ruminants—or, to quote the Bible, those creatures that "part the hoof and chew the cud." These would include deer, elk, sheep, goats, bison and antelope.

Q. Then how do ruminants get their food?

A. Instead of a good set of uppers in front, the ruminant has a tough palate and a prehensile tongue. Grasping a bunch of twigs or grass, the animal presses the food against the roof of its mouth and tears the clump away with a twist of the head. In the process the critter may use its tongue somewhat as you'd use your mittened hand.

Q. Why does a cow have four stomachs?

A. The four compartments of the stomach of cattle and other ruminants might be handy in our own hurry-up way of life. They allow their owners to eat and run.

With such a division of alimentary labor, great amounts of food can be consumed rapidly. Leaves, grass and twigs are high in fiber content so they need a lot of chewing. The various stomach compartments not only store them but help moisten and partially break them down by bacterial and enzyme action. Then the animal, having packed its lunch, so to speak, can re-

RONALD ROOD

tire to the safety of some secluded spot. It passes up a bolus, or cud, from the proper stomach compartment, and finishes its meal at leisure.

Q. Why does a bull get mad when it sees red?

A. It doesn't get mad. No more than when it sees any other color, that is. Actually, bulls most frequently injure people who are wearing white. This is because herdsmen and others working around cattle often wear white coveralls.

Which brings to mind the old saw that no bull will injure you when you're carrying a big red flag—if you carry it fast enough.

Q. In feeding my animals I discovered some moldy hay. Rather than take a chance, I discarded it. Would it have hurt them?

A. Molds and their spores are found almost everywhere. They are a part of normal living. Occasionally certain types cause problems if they invade the bodies of people or animals. Without knowing the species of mold it is hard to say what its effect would be, but as the mold has utilized edible portions of the plant for its own growth, the feed was probably low in nutritive value anyway. Add to this the tendency of animals to refuse to eat moldy food and you were probably correct in tossing it out.

Q. What about moldy bread or other table food?

A. The mold you see is only the visible collection of fruiting bodies springing from a larger mass of threads known as a mycelium. These threads may extend, unseen, a long distance through the rest of the food. In cheese and some well-aged meats the presence of certain molds imparts a desirable flavor. Doubtless you have been eating mold, in one way or another, most of your life—even if you've carefully trimmed the visible portion from the food.

Q. How can I tell a non-poisonous mushroom from a poisonous one?

A. There is no single certain way. Even the sense of taste— if you get that far—can fool you. Some poisonous species have an excellent flavor. On the other hand, plenty of edible mushrooms never grace anybody's table because they're about as tasty as a corncob.

Q. I'm interested in edible natural foods. I came across a wild strawberry patch. Would it be worth the effort to try to take a few plants home and tame them?

A. Your question is one I've continually asked myself as I wandered through the countryside. Whether it's strawberries, or cherries, or some other delicious-looking plant, the answer is that you'll probably be disappointed. After all, most cultivated fruit has been painstakingly developed from the wild variety. There's probably a better potential crop awaiting in your seed catalogue or the local nursery.

Q. Suppose I want to dig up a wild plant. Any suggestions?

A. Yes. Start by getting permission. Then take plenty of soil. Try to duplicate natural conditions as much as possible. Have the same amount of shade, moisture, general temperature and exposure conditions. Stake the plant up if necessary. Water it well until it becomes established.

Q. When is the best time to transplant?

A. Generally speaking, when the plant is dormant. If this is not possible, try to wait until flower and fruiting seasons have passed. These drain enough energy from the plant without adding the shock of digging and resetting.

Q. What shrubs are best to plant for wildlife food?

A. A plant that bears a good annual crop of fruit and holds it well into the winter is a good bet. It is usually more useful than one that produces only occasionally or drops its fruit early. Use local plants where possible: they'll probably stand your climate better. Your county Agricultural Extension Service has bulletins about plants suited to your area.

Q. How can I keep a Christmas tree from shedding its needles?

A. Various leaf-retaining chemicals are sold on the market. Some seem to be effective; some do not. Here are a few suggestions:

84 RONALD ROOD

Select a freshly cut tree, if possible. Get one that is a little longer than you need. Saw off the bottom few inches of the old, dried wood. Pare the bark away above this cut to a height of two or three inches. Quickly immerse this skinned portion in water, or at least wrap it in a wet rag. Keep it wet—never let it dry out, not even once.

Place the tree in water deep enough to cover the de-barked section well. Maintain the height of water so this exposed wood is always immersed. The tree will take up a quart or more a day, depending on its size. Keep the room cool, if possible. Do not place the tree near a radiator or in direct sunlight.

And there you have a green, fragrant tree that will stay fresh for as long as you need it. Not only that, but the wallpaper may stop peeling and the chair joints may stop creaking. Your *Tannenbaum*, it seems, will act as a natural humidifier.

Q. Why do some flowers bloom at night?

A. The obvious answer is so that they may be fertilized by moths and night-flying insects. In this way a biological niche is filled. Scientists are still at odds as to which came first: did the flowers open at night because there were moths, or did the moths choose the hours of darkness because there were flowers waiting for them? It's a chicken-and-egg situation.

Q. Flowers have many colors, but I have heard that bees are partially color blind. Explain.

A. The honeybee can see most colors, but it is apparently insensitive to red. The few wild flowers that are true red may be fertilized by other insects. The reds of many of our cultivated varieties are the result of careful breeding and selection.

Q. A friend in Colorado says some people will not wear red because of the hummingbirds. Does it make the birds mad?

A. A common species in parts of the West is the broad-tailed hummingbird. When it flies its rapid wing beat makes a buzzing sound. As with many hummingbirds, this species is strongly attracted to red. It visits red flowers and "feeder" vials containing red-tinted sugar water—plus red kerchiefs, hats and other clothing. To be closely investigated by a loudly buzzing creature intent on finding a little nectar must be disconcerting, to say the least.

I used to enjoy the letters from students who wanted help with their science projects. Such were the boy who wondered how to go about developing tail-less mice "before our biology fair in April," and another lad who needed advice on how to stuff a turkey. Not Thanksgiving stuffing—taxidermy stuffing.

One sixth-grader, straight-faced, asked what biological processes went on after dark and "how can I demonstrate them?" An enterprising girl on the Oregon coast had decided to cut a starfish in half for her study: "then what do I do?" A thousand miles to the south, in San Diego, another girl hoped we'd help her to "control sex in a rabbit." She gave no further explanation. After all, that was supposed to be *our* problem.

I did a double-take when I got a request from a boy in Ohio who wanted to set up a display of poisonous plants "for the audience to handle and taste." One of his feminine classmates wrote in because her project involved "showing the various hallucinogenic plants and how they can be identified in Ohio." Now, *that* could have been quite a science fair!

Sometimes, as in the case of that girl and her forbidden fruit, I had to try to nudge a project into different channels. One of the commonest of such efforts seemed to involve maltreatment of animals in the interest of science. I have had requests for information on how to set up a starvation diet, and how to demonstrate the effect of soft drinks on the teeth by feeding nothing but soda pop to guinea pigs. One student wanted information about "some of the foods that are great sources of cholesterol, because I need to feed them to a rabbit to show how bad they are."

An eighth-grader hoped we'd tell him what apparatus he'd need to show the loudest sound an animal could endure. A girl wanted suggestions about "the kinds of distorting diseases I could inject into eggs that would show on the embryo. If it is not possible for me to use diseases, then would you send me

　　　　　　　　　　　　RONALD ROOD

information on chemicals I could inject in the egg that would have effect on the embryo. I would like to use several chemicals, to show several reactions."

As such questions came to me and I had to answer them, I realized how far we have strayed in our worship of science. These few requests were just the tiny skim from the top, so to speak. How many thousands of victims are sacrificed senselessly each year by earnest, sincere students in their search for truth? How many creatures are starved and maimed, how many baby chicks injected, just out of curiosity or because somebody needs a demonstration?

Yet much good can come of it. From the thousands of curiosity-seekers arise the scientists of tomorrow: the sensitive, compassionate men and women who have brought new blessings into the lives of people and animals because once they, too, wondered.

I recall being curious about the nutritional value of a certain fruit in the brushlands about the University of Connecticut, for instance. So I set up an experiment involving this fruit—the common bayberry—and half a dozen pheasants. The idea was to see if a bayberry diet would maintain their lives through the cold months of winter. Day after day I fed those gray, waxy berries the size of air-rifle shot to my six birds. Daily I watched the pheasants waste away.

Finally, one morning, the handsome cock pheasant was dead. The glistening green of his head and neck, the burnished bronze of his breast, the delicate barring and mottling of a thousand feathers—all lay beneath a funeral shroud of a quarter-inch of new snow drawn gently over him sometime during the night.

His ordeal was over. And so, I vowed, was that of the remaining hen pheasants. Seized by a monstrous remorse, I trudged a mile to the supply room at the wildlife management lab. Picking out a bag of the best feed, I took it back to the pheasant pens. Then, during the next few weeks I watched in relief as those five hens recovered to abundant good health. Taking them out to a spot where I had heard a wild cock crowing, I let them go.

Had that unfortunate male been wasted? Not, I determined, if I could help it. More than one winter food station has been set out in his name. Many a magazine article aimed at helping us know the exquisite perfection of the wild world has been silently dedicated to that huddled form beneath its frosty coverlet. And now you, too, may carry out some act of kindness because you know about him.

But enough of the seamy side of science. Let me share half a dozen quickies with you. Then I'll let you have a hand at answering a few for yourself.

One reader wondered if there's an animal that stuns other animals with sound waves, for instance. Doubtless the long-suffering parents of a few million rock music fans would have a ready answer. But on searching, I found that he probably was referring to a crustacean known as the pistol shrimp. This creature snaps its claw with such force that it creates a shock wave in the water. Its neighbors suffer as from a physical blow. Put a pistol shrimp in a glass aquarium, let it snap, and you think the glass has cracked.

A Pennsylvania fisherman wondered if male earthworms were better than females as bait. I had to confess there was no difference. None at all: both sexes are present in each worm.

A Brooklyn scout found a turtle at summer camp. Bringing it home, he got to wondering if it was a boy or a girl, so he passed the problem along to us. Look at the lower shell, or plastron, I suggested. If it bulged slightly it was probably a female, because she needed the space between those unyielding decks to develop a dozen or more eggs.

The male, on the other hand, would tend to have a slightly concave plastron. This would allow him to walk without bumping his underside as he traveled. Also, being practical, it was a handy way to help him keep his place atop the smoothly convex shell of the female during the act of mating.

A lad in Michigan had heard that bat droppings, or guano, were a valuable and high-priced source of fertilizer. He asked us for suggestions on how to make a device to collect it as it was deposited. After no small amount of searching, I found plans for a gadget that might work, and sent him a copy of the drawings and specifications.

That first question was a bit unusual, but his second one floored me. "Thank you for your information," he said. "Now I wonder if you can tell me where I might find some bats."

A Texan wondered if it was true that there were more cattle in Texas than in any other state. Doubtless he already knew: there are. A North Dakotan wondered if hogs perspire. They don't: they pant like a dog. They also wallow in nice, cooling mud.

"My beagle [wrote a man in central Vermont] runs rabbits all the time. Now I'd like to teach him to run deer. How should I do this?"

I answered—without letting him know that my home was about fifteen miles away—that it's against the law in Vermont for dogs to run deer.

Now here are those questions I've promised you. How would *you* answer them?

"We note with regret that our set of encyclopedias does not

include any information on the cobia, or sergeant fish. A friend of ours has this data in a much cheaper set she bought in a supermarket. Do you have any explanation as to this omission? Needless to say we were disturbed to find our set inadequate."

"If the length of your neck affects the tone of your voice, why doesn't the giraffe say anything? I should think he would at least be able to make a loud moo."

"How do worms talk with each other?"

"Kindly send me whatever information is available on the Economic Importance of the Moth."

"How do birds tell the time of day, and how do you know?"

"Does the male bear sleep or does he run around all winter?"

"Please send me points suitable for proving that barbarians are happier than civilized people."

RONALD ROOD

"Please send me a ten-minute report on the creation of the world."

"Which way does a dog wag his tail—left or right—on the first wag?"

"What is the difference between a duck and other fowls that causes the duck to be lovable with people and other animals and fowls?"

"The only thing you tell about the chipmunk is that the mating period is in May. I should think you'd be more interested in chipmunks than that."

"My aunt and uncle are clam diggers. Can you tell me what they eat?"

"Would you please send me a complete list of information on the jackrabbit in the Western states. I have been told they are as big as a deer and jump fifty or sixty feet, and would like to know if this is true."

"My uncle told me that a camel was really a horse that was put together by a committee. What does he mean?"

And so on. And on, and on. Now that you've sampled those nearly twelve thousand requests, you must have the general idea. There is nothing like a little curiosity.

Except, perhaps, the things you have to dig up to satisfy it.

5. *Playback*

It's been fifteen years since I answered my last encyclopedia letter, but the mailbox has not been empty. Bill McKean, the rural mail carrier you've already met, sees to that. Daily he leaves a good handful of cards and letters. Among them are always one or two from people I've never met, but who share my interest in the world of the outdoors.

Perhaps they've read something in a newspaper, or have seen an interesting television program. Perhaps they have an idea they hope I can use in a book. Often they have a question to ask. No matter what the reason for writing, there are those letters in my mailbox—nearly two hours' worth of correspondence daily.

I look forward to those letters nearly as much as if I were a homesick G.I. at Mail Call. The chance to swap yarns and learn about the experiences of others is a welcome relief from the hours I must spend snooping through reference books and chasing down some elusive fact. To me, this is one of the greatest rewards of writing: the chance to make new friends through the printed word.

These friends are of many sizes and ages. Their letters are endlessly interesting. Just as with those twelve thousand research requests, no two are exactly alike. Sometimes the writer will volunteer an account of a meeting with some wild animal. Other times the letter includes a sketch, a photograph, a poem. Occasionally a feather or a flower or a leaf will fall from the envelope. Not always a little gift, though: sometimes it's part of a mystery, and can I furnish the name of the appropriate bird or plant?

One youthful entrepreneur who should go far in this world asked me to visit her fourth-grade class in Kenosha, Wisconsin. She hadn't checked with her teacher, but it would be all right, she assured me. "And which day would you like to come, Mr. Rood?"

I wrote back, thanked her for the invitation, and suggested that she get in touch with her teacher just in case something else might be planned for the day. Apparently something *was* planned, as I have not had any further word. But it's such youthful enthusiasm that makes each of Bill McKean's daily offerings at my mailbox seem like a Christmas stocking.

The students of one junior high class, in a transport of enthusiasm over *Hundred Acre Welcome*, a book I'd done about a wild Chincoteague pony we'd brought to Vermont from Virginia, wrote me twenty-three individual letters. Part of each letter was a sketch, laboriously drawn and colored, which depicted some event in the book.

Those kids had done their homework. I was delighted to answer each letter personally, and I felt warm and friendly for days.

One children's book is the result of those years as a research editor. It lists the prize-winners in many lines of endeavor: the highest jumper, the fastest runner, the deepest diver, and so on. A sprinkling of letters is from readers, young and old, who write to tell me that (1) they find it hard to believe a record they've seen in the book, or (2) they've got a better one. I jot down their new record or go back over the figures for the old one—and thank my stars that I'd done *my* homework, too.

A girl in Kentucky sent her copy of the animal champions book, asking if I'd write something in the front of it. Then, as an afterthought to her request, she penned this little comment:

"It is nice to know about animals with all these records, but can't people do *anything* best?"

Yes, apparently they can. Although deer can outjump us, fish can outswim us, the clumsiest barnyard duck can outfly us, there are two areas where we shine. For all our poor showing in the realm of athletic ability, we can outthink other creatures, of course—and we can outlast them.

Many people live to be a hundred, I told my small friend. However, with the possible exception of the giant tortoises, there seem to be no centenarians among wild animals. The hazards of life are so keen that old age is seldom a problem. There are eagles and parrots that live fifty years, yes—but these have

RONALD ROOD

been sheltered in captivity. "Even a wrinkled old elephant," I concluded, "may reach little more than half a century."

Questions like that one tend to keep me on my toes. So do the rare—and luckily so—letters from readers who figure they've found a mistake. Even though long hours of study and many pages of notes go into the smallest magazine article, errors still can creep in. If I don't discover a flaw while there's yet time to take it out, someone will catch it after it's too late. And then I get a letter.

Reading such a letter, I feel a mounting sense of discomfort. Rushing to the printed story, I open it to the offending page. And there, staring at me, is the Big Mistake.

It's a sobering thought, the permanence of the printed word. What you and I say together in a conversation is lost on the wind. Recordings and photographs can be erased and retouched. But once it's down in black and white, it's permanent. Even if it's wrong.

A number of years ago, for instance, I had an article on snakes in *Vermont Life* Magazine. The story garnered a variety of responses. Some were from people who know snakes as normal, inoffensive Vermont natives. Other letters were from resort owners who were afraid the very mention of the reptiles would hurt their business. I replied as best I could to each letter, put them in the thick folder of notes I had collected on the subject and filed the whole works away.

Several years later, a selection of the magazine's nature articles were published as a book. This revived the snakes and brought more letters. One of them came clear from Honolulu. What did I mean, the gentleman asked, by saying that a mother snake did not swallow her young for their protection? He'd seen it happen. He had surprised one happy family as it was sunning on a rock when he was a boy in New England. As he watched, the mother put every one of the babies down the hatch where it would be safe.

Hm–m–m. It was hard to contradict an eyewitness account.

Especially one hallowed by the charm of boyhood memories. But I had to give it a try.

The whole key to the persistent myth about the mother-baby story is that it takes place *for the infants' protection.* "Do you recall that they came out again?" I wrote back. "In other words, did you see them make that U–turn?"

Well, he replied, no. Come to think of it, all he saw was a big snake swallowing little ones. Perhaps (and I could see the wheels turning in his head as he wrote) the big one was merely hungry?

And so I was lucky on that one. However, all it takes is one such letter to keep me honest, so to speak. You've probably said it yourself: "It must be so—I read it in a book."

One earlier time I was not so fortunate. In my first book, no less, I made an error. Right there on the second page. It was an error of one small word, but once discovered it practically glittered.

In an effort to set the scene for the book I had mentioned the animals on our farm. We had raised a pig for meat and had it hanging in the barn, head and feet still attached "but the hair taken off." Or that's what I meant to say. When the book came out, however, the word didn't read "hair" at all. It read "hide."

Of course there's a vast difference between the two. Nobody I know has ever taken the hide off a newly killed pig. Nor have we, in half a dozen such performances here, or back when I was a youngster on the farm.

What does such a detail matter? Plenty—if you know anything about farming. And Sam Ogden, out of his long years of farm experience, noticed the mistake at once. Samuel Ogden, whose writings I had long admired and whose penetrating comments could do so much for—or to—a book, had decided to review *Land Alive.* If he needed any ammunition, there it was, right on page two.

And there it was, as well, early in his review. Did this new writer fancy himself a farmer? If so, he practiced farming differently from any farmer Sam had known—and then he recalled some of his own experiences. His remarks remained gentle, however, although he might easily have pointed out that a single flaw could make the reader suspect the whole book.

When I finished reading the review, I realized that a seasoned writer had called this fresh beginner to task. But not harshly. I thanked him inwardly, and resolved to do a better job of proofreading in the future.

Score two for the old professionals. The first time had been that cicada article in which I'd scattered the insects all over Long Island where they didn't belong. Now I had inadvertently skinned a pig—and had left it in that deplorable condition through two proofreadings. Next time I'd put research *and* double-checking together. Then maybe I'd have a winning combination.

Apparently Sam's remarks made potential readers curious. "I bought your book," one lady confided, "just because I wanted to see what Mr. Ogden was talking about."

Now, I decided, if I could only get it banned in Boston . . .

Book reviewers, flooded as they may be with offerings from hopeful authors and publishers, can find themselves short of time. Under such a circumstance there's a tendency, I suspect, to warm over somebody else's remarks, add a word of your own, and scurry in under the deadline. Such, I hope, was the case with a review that I clipped and have hanging on the wall near my typewriter:

"Mr. Rood's book [it says] is well spoken of by some who know it."

Another bit of faint praise came from a girl who enclosed a check in her letter. "If you send me a copy of your book," she said, "I promise I will read it."

Then, perhaps in an effort to soften that remark, she added another: "You see, I have to have it for a book report."

Her letter took me back to my own days of teaching. Nearly every teacher has enjoyed those occasional moments of what I called "playback"—when you realize the students are totally caught up by the topic at hand. It's an indefinable Something that makes all the difference between a ho-hum class and one that's a delight for everybody. With a few good teachers it must occur frequently, while with a few at the other end of the scale it may hardly ever happen.

In my own classes those rare moments were signaled to me in many ways. A student—or, perhaps a whole roomful—shows by some subtle change that what was merely polite classroom manners has become rapt attention. Sometimes a student would interrupt me in mid-sentence with a blurted-out observation that drove home the point I was trying to make. I didn't mind the interjection at all. In fact, I was grateful. It showed we were both on a common track.

Some of my liking for teaching must have carried over into my writing, for I began to get playback there, too. People responded to my experiences with observations of their own. Reading about that controversial pig, for instance, one boy in North Carolina volunteered that "pigs make good eating, unless they are pets. Ours was and it wasn't."

Another reader, perhaps hoping I could reverse the normal march of events, told me she had been looking for a pig as a household pet—"one that starts out small and stays small. What kind of pig is Li'l Abner's 'Salomey,' for instance?"

Other domestic animals figured in correspondence in interesting ways. A boy who had apparently been promising himself to write to me felt obliged to explain the delay. "I am sorry I have not written to you sooner," he said, "but I have been very busy. My cat had kittens."

A pre-teen girl brought me up to date on the adventures of herself, her friend, and her horse—I think:

"Dear Mr. Rood, My girl friend has a horse. Her name is Anny. She is a orphan. Her mother was sold to a man."

One small correspondent told me "my hobby is animals and returnables." Another, perhaps finding that small animals are *not* returnable, confessed that he had been trying to raise a baby bird, "but it died after the cat ate it."

A New Jersey cat, apparently less lucky in encounters with other animals, occasioned this recital from a fifth-grader:

"Dubby must have got in a fight because he was bleeding in his hind legs. Also his intestines were clogged up and he couldn't go to the bathroom. He might have been embarrassed because he ran away."

Other pets prompted other letters, from "my Saint Bernard puppy who is no saint" to an unusual tropical fish that a man discovered in his large community aquarium. He described it as best he could, finishing by suggesting that since there were many fish in the tank it "might possibly be the result of cross-pollination."

As one book of mine followed another, those letters increased in number. A tale about an orphan porcupine we raised to maturity brought forth a number of requests as to how readers might get a porky of their own. That book about the wild pony colt who had traveled with us in our car from Virginia to our hundred acres in Vermont resulted in the same type of question from horse-lovers. A book on pet care precipitated requests on a variety of subjects ranging from de-scenting skunks (don't: if you can't stand 'em, don't have 'em) to getting a wild animal for a pet (also don't: they may become possessions, but never pets—besides, in many states it's against the law).

I was encouraged by one girl to "Please write. Here is my address if you know how to hold a rabbit." A friend of mine whose young son arrived home one day with an orphan woodchuck, wondered how to stop it from chasing cats, while an observant third-grader informed me that "I found some acorn shells. Do you think there is a squirrel?"

One youthful correspondent had an anolis, or American chameleon, which he had brought to Massachusetts from Georgia. In the summer it ate flies and other insects, but these were hard to find in Boston in the winter. Did I have any ideas that would help?

I thanked him for his interest, made a couple of suggestions, packed my reply in the stamped envelope he had thoughtfully enclosed, and mailed it back to Boston. That, I figured, would be the last I'd hear from him.

I was mistaken. The self-addressed envelope should have tipped me off: such consideration is a rarity indeed. Now he was writing to express his thanks. As I opened his letter I failed to recognize the name right away, but its contents soon refreshed my memory. "Dear Mr. Rood," it began, "I thought I might tell you that I got mealworms . . . "

Where else but in a naturalist's mail?

Sometimes a letter turns a familiar word to a new use. A Florida schoolboy wrote about a snake that had been killed on the highway. "It was dead," he told me, "but it was still moving. Probably it was nervous."

A worried housewife, concerned about millipedes on the floors and in the hall, wondered if she should have the house "exterminated." And a girl scout, headed for camp, asked for suggestions as to "how I can contract the poison of poison ivy."

I was tempted to write back, "Nothing to it; it's easy." However, knowing that she really meant "counteract," I gave her a few suggestions and wished her happy camping.

Occasionally the mail is too slow, even if it's airmail. A letter from a gentleman who wonders what to feed an orphaned chipmunk whose eyes are still closed requires more than an answer by return mail. He and his small boarder doubtless needed help before he sat down to write the letter. Perhaps it's beyond the point of no return already, but I give him a phone call anyway.

As it turned out, that telephone call was too late. Not that the 'munk had expired, but the man and his wife had figured out a feeding program by themselves. "Chippy's doing fine," the woman told me cheerfully. "We decided he was sort of a cross between a guinea pig and a hamster, and we've had babies of both."

Two more new friends. No—make that three.

Sometimes people telephone me instead of writing. A lady in Oklahoma called to ask what to do with three baby birds. In five minutes the two of us had hit upon a solution.

Another woman in Mississippi had a pet turtle whose shell was becoming soft; we figured out the answer to that one, too: put a bit of calcium-rich cuttlebone in the water in its tank.

A vacationer had a skunk under the cabin—obviously an occasion for a phone call. Answer: (1) Don't panic. (2) Put something tasty, like a chicken neck, outside on the ground. (3) Try a discreet closing of a door or plugging of an entrance when the skunk is out. (4) If all else fails, no need to worry, anyway: skunks rarely use their weapons in close quarters. Besides, they're great mousers, anyway.

One couple, hearing a strange cry in the night, found themselves at a loss as to its identity. Getting me on the phone, they held the instrument out the window. Luckily, it was a sound I had heard in the woods behind my house, and I was familiar

with it. So, across the miles, the three of us listened together to the notes of a saw-whet owl.

Telephone callers sometimes offer me gifts, as well. "There's this baby squirrel," they'll begin on a nice spring day—and I know what's coming. Since I've raised and cared for other creatures, they wonder, couldn't I sort of sandwich in one more squirrel?

If the phone call is in the autumn, their generosity takes a slightly different turn. Little Ricky—now Big Rick—nipped two of the kids, tangled with the dog, and terrorized an insurance man. Up there on my hundred acres of Lincoln land, wouldn't there be some place they could give a raccoon its freedom?

Once each such telephone call meant a new little crisis to be met and mastered. But no more. Now it's simple. In self-defense I joined the board of directors of the Discovery Museum in Essex Junction, Vermont, some two dozen miles from our home. This museum is a busy place, with cages and pens and animal runs. Such enclosures serve as hostels for a succession of creatures, temporarily down on their luck, until they're well enough to be let go.

I suggest that my caller take a trip to the Discovery Museum. It'll be a good experience, I figure. Take Raging Rick along, of course; there'll be a place for him. And give me a telephone call next week to let me know how things came out. In this way I have at least postponed the ultimate problem—sort of like putting used razor blades into a slot in a hotel-room wall.

Wonderful people, all of them, with their letters and phone calls. I treasure every one. I just hope the good folks who may recognize their efforts here will take them with the same spirit of fun as they're imparted. After all, without those letters and telephone calls I'd never know what happened to my efforts after they had gone to the newsstands and the booksellers. It helps little to be a writer if there are no readers.

As I type these last words, Peg has just come in from the mailbox. She has an armload of the day's offerings. If I'm lucky, there'll be a few items for the writer in me. Together we'll read them and agree, perhaps, on what to give for an answer.

Then I'll seat myself before this noisy old typewriter and begin the part of writing that I like best: my daily two hours of playback.

6.   Unaccustomed
as I Am . . .

I owe a big debt to a man and a boy from Rutland. A debt of gratitude and not a little money. Yet I don't even know their names.

The two were a father-and-son combination from a scout troop. They materialized at my door one Sunday afternoon. "We're supposed to get a speaker for our annual Dads' Night banquet," the boy said. "So my father and I wondered if you'd come and talk to us."

In my teaching days I had spoken before hundreds of classes. I had had a bunch of Sunday school youngsters for a couple of years, too. But these had been captive audiences, more or less. What kind of a performance was expected of me at a father-son dinner where everybody was supposed to have a good time?

"Well—thanks," I said, wondering what I could use for a topic. "But what would you want me to talk about?"

"Oh, anything you choose."

"Anything?"

"Sure. You know, animals, or camping, or wildlife. Something from your new book, maybe."

At least they gave me plenty of latitude. An ex-teacher shouldn't lack for words, I figured. I could probably find a few stories about the funny thing that happened to me on the way to the banquet. Then I could add one or two of my own experiences—like the night we slept out under the stars on an Iowa prairie and awoke to find ourselves the center of a circle of hundreds of curious white-faced cattle. Or the time John White and I went on a camping trip for two, got to telling ghost stories around the fire, and scared ourselves right out of the woods.

Maybe it'd be fun. In fact, why not? So I consulted my date book—which I knew very well to be empty. "Fine," I told them after a suitable pause. "I'll be there."

That was my first speaking engagement. I don't remember, now, what funny thing happened on the way to the banquet. Nor do I recall what I told them besides those two camping stories. All I know is that those kids and their dads were in a jovial mood after a good meal, and the whole lot of us had a great time.

It was the best talk I ever gave. Best for me, at least. Not that the speech itself was so wonderful, but it opened the door to a new world. Here, I discovered, was a chance to get out and meet the people I enjoyed.

Even with just a single book behind me at that point, I was aware of how solitary a task writing can be. Although you're communing with people, you have to shut them out of your life. At least temporarily. For the duration of the book or the magazine article it's just you and that typewriter—or pen, or pencil, or however you get the job done.

Not that other persons cannot be around. It's seldom as bad

as that. It's just that they cannot have much to do with me—nor I with them—while some literary gem is being fashioned.

Peg can turn the radio or television on in second gear, or play the piano in the next room with the door open, and it doesn't bother me at all. She can even carry on a conversation with a friend and I'll scarcely hear it.

A normal conversation, that is. But let them drop their voices confidentially, and I begin to listen. Pretty soon I'm straining my ears to get every word—and there goes my writing effort.

That visit with the boy scouts was a welcome relief from the clattering of this old Underwood No. 5 typewriter. Not only that, but it was an education. As William Lyon Phelps told our college graduating class, "Although I've been in school almost constantly since I was three, there's not a first-grader alive who cannot tell me *something*."

That's how I felt, too, at that first talk. I've been feeling that way ever since. When you exchange ideas with people of similar interests it's much better, I figure, than merely swapping items at a hobby show. You've got every one of the ideas you started with, plus the new thoughts of the people you meet. That night in Rutland I listened to several camping yarns and made a host of new friends. Besides, I was refreshed by the boundless enthusiasm of those wonderful kids.

So I owe a great deal to that boy and his dad. They got me started. Now, when the telephone rings, there's a knock on the door, or I get a letter bearing the words "We wondered if you would be available . . . " I greet the opportunity with joy.

Would I be available? Try to stop me! Even if I seldom come away from one lecture with enough material for another, I'm still much the richer for it. I'll at least have had a change of scene.

I always get a chuckle, too. People are just that much fun. One time, early in our years here in Lincoln, I asked Gilbert Goodyear to bring his tractor and equipment to help remove

RONALD ROOD

the winter's accumulation deposited by our family cow and a couple of horses.

"Sure," he said. "Be around as soon as I can. Now I wonder if you could do *me* a favor."

The tradition of "trading work" is an ancient one in New England—you help me and I'll help you. So I asked Gilbert what was on his mind.

"Well," he said, "since I'm your neighbor here in Lincoln, I'm supposed to find out if you'd speak at our graduation."

The day was free, I discovered. So I told him to sign me up.

A few weeks later the big day arrived. That evening, Holley Hall in Bristol echoed the measured beat of "Pomp and Circumstance" as three dozen high school seniors marched up to take their places on the platform. The time came for my talk; I gave it and sat down.

After the ceremonies, as the graduates were filing out past me, Gilbert paused. No doubt he was going to congratulate me on a fine speech, I decided.

Not so. Just a little unfinished business. "I ain't forgotten you, Mr. Rood," he said. "Be up to take out that manure pretty soon."

Cause and effect? I hope not.

Another memorable graduation came after I'd written a book for children. A friend of mine asked if I'd speak at her daughter's eighth-grade commencement exercises "since you've written a book, Ron, and they all like to read."

I had taught school long enough to have my doubts about the last part of that statement, but I went to the ceremony anyway.

As is often the case with such exercises in a small town, the graduation was too good an occasion to let go by lightly. There were recitations, the awarding of prizes for best, second-best and third-best in all the grades; several selections by the school orchestra—with echoes from its diapered younger siblings in the crowded hall—and a recital by the pupils of a local

piano teacher. Following this talent bonanza, I was to say a few well-chosen words.

As the evening wore on and the hall got hotter, in prospect my speech got shorter and shorter. When the time came for the piano recital it had almost vanished.

I recall little of the first two or three piano solos. Then came a dream of a little girl right out of a Shirley Temple movie: starched crinoline dress, white tights, shiny patent-leather shoes. A ripple of delight went through the audience as she marched over to the piano and sat down.

She began to play. Clearly and in perfect time, the music tinkled forth under the charm of those dainty fingers. But then, suddenly, she stopped. She had forgotten her notes.

While the audience waited uneasily, she stared at her hands. They wouldn't respond, however, so she went back a few

RONALD ROOD

measures. Starting again she came to the offending portion of the piece—and halted at the same place.

This would never do. Going back to the beginning, she gave the whole thing another try. It went along splendidly, and everything was fine—until she hit the rough spot. Then she faltered to a stop once more.

She turned from the piano. Rising to her full four-foot-four in that crinkly dress, she looked at the audience. Then she took a deep breath, gave a resounding Bronx cheer—and flounced off the stage.

The place collapsed in pandemonium.

After that, the rest of the program didn't matter. I hardly recall whether the eighth-graders graduated or not—or whether I gave my abbreviated speech. But I'll remember the little girl and that grammar school commencement long after I've forgotten all the advice given and received at a score of graduations.

"Upstaging," it's called, when another person on the platform steals the scene. In my college days with the drama club, upstaging was nearly the worst thing a performer could do. It's almost as bad as forgetting your lines. But when you're trying to get far away from that noisy typewriter in a quiet room back home the whole affair can be delightful.

It hardly matters how it happens. Whether it's a spunky little girl in a daffodil dress who stops the show, or somebody else on the program who falls flat and brings the house down at the same time, it's all in fun. Since writing is such a lonesome job, I value a good laugh with people, even if it's on me.

Sometimes it comes so fast it makes you blink. I recall one dinner when I was seated beside the master of ceremonies, an irrepressible prankster. Since I knew he'd appreciate a joke, I tried one out on him as we were eating. He replied with one of his own. These led to more, and so on until I laughed so hard I spilled the coffee. When he got up to introduce me there was a gleam of mischief in his eye.

" . . . And here," he concluded after a few brief remarks,

"is Ronald Rood—one of the funniest persons you'll ever meet!"

Then, sitting down, he folded his arms as if to say, "Now, let's see you get out of *that* one!"

It might have been really tough to live up to such a build-up —if we hadn't just been swapping jokes. But I got even with him quick: I told two of his best stories.

Not always, of course, can you find such a comeback. One day I was supposed to speak right after a luncheon, but found myself pressed for time because of a telephone call. "Sandy," I told the woman who was presiding, "I'm sorry, but something unexpected has come up. Any chance we could reverse the usual order and have my talk before lunch instead of after?"

She was wonderfully understanding. It'd be no trouble at all; the noon meal was a buffet luncheon anyway, and a few more minutes wouldn't matter.

Sandy was understanding, yes. She explained the change to the group before whom I was to speak. But she brought me up short with her final comment:

" . . . So we'll hear from Mr. Rood," she said, "and then we'll enjoy ourselves."

There was also the time I was presented to the League of Vermont Writers by my friend Lilian Carlisle. In this case we had just finished a magnificent meal, and the best thing I could think of was for everyone to find an easy chair. However, the program had to go on. So, in an effort to reflect the general feeling of comfort and well-being around the room, Lilian polished me off by saying, "Ron, I just hope I don't fall asleep during your talk."

This brought a laugh. Realizing what she'd said, she hastened to correct it. "What I mean," she added hastily, "is that we've already *had* our good time—"

More laughs. "—Up to now!" she finished.

Of course there is always the danger of drowsing after a

hearty meal. One time the waitress came around with the coffee, asking if I wanted my cup refilled.

"You bet," I answered, with a wink at one of the other guests at the head table. "I've got to stay awake—I'm the speaker."

My companion immediately rose to the occasion. "That's so, isn't it?" he said, in sudden recognition of the fact. "In that case, pour me another cup, too!"

People do all sorts of things to keep themselves occupied during a talk. Women bring their knitting. Men inspect their fingernails. Both sexes polish their glasses and doodle on a piece of paper. I've seen people reorganize their wallets, write letters, draw pictures. One lady, who apparently had been forewarned about a certain speaker, sat next to me with a big box of trading stamps. Solemnly she licked them all, placed them in books—and finished just in time to applaud when the speaker was through.

The person who's doing two things at the same time is just one of the public speaker's occupational hazards. Now and again the person on the platform cries "enough." Once I watched as a missionary, recently returned from the Orient, drew a great curved sword and brandished it above the startled audience—probably causing the event to be recorded in the stitchery of half a dozen scarves, mittens and other projects. However, having more than once brought along my own knitting, so to speak, I know the feeling of accomplishment you can get. Besides, as one of our town selectmen told me when I complained about the apparent divided attention through the audience, "Don't worry, Ron. And don't take it personal. It just gives them something to think about while you're talking."

There are other perils of the platform. They may advance to meet you, crouch during your talk, and even await your departure. Just as a formal business meeting is run according to a traditional schedule and is subject to procedures known as

Robert's Rules of Order, there seems to be a set of regulations peculiarly adapted to the discomfiture of the guest speaker. Peg, having seen these regulations in operation several times, suggests that they be called Ronald's Rules of Disorder.

Here are half a dozen of them:

1. *The Helping Hands.* As soon as you arrive, the H.H.'s are there. Whether it's one cherub or a host of cherubim and their elders, they operate according to a most commendable principle: they want to give you a lift. I am grateful for their presence, but their enthusiasm can be a bit upsetting. Literally.

There you are, pulling up in front of the auditorium. The back seat of the car is full of projectors, slides, books, and a quarter-mile of extension cord. The minute you get out, a flying wedge of Helping Hands advances to welcome you. While some of them divert your attention, the rest attempt to divest your back seat of that paraphernalia. If you're carrying anything there is apt to be a silent struggle for possession of it. Thus greeted, you are convoyed to the door.

Don't get me wrong. I love the members of the Order of the Helping Hand. I feel strangely alone if they're not there. However, until I learned to anticipate their presence, I felt not a little uneasy as I watched a precious projector go careening through the doorway, perhaps banging into something before it disappeared. Nor will I forget the time I neglected to put the locking ring securely on top of a carousel of slides. A youthful helper, eager to assist me, picked up the carousel— and promptly dropped it. Both of us watched in fascination as the carousel rolled away, distributing slides in a perfect pattern down the aisle.

I have had books dropped, carefully wound extension cords pulled out into a tangle, and my hat and coat spirited away before I knew which way they'd gone. Although the H.H.'s did it, it's really my fault. For it's up to me to channel all that energy.

Now, twenty years wiser than when I began, I try to arrive

early so I can unload at my leisure. But since I know how disappointed a welcoming committee can be if it cannot do something, I start by handing out an object that's sturdy and helperproof. Thus the fragile items are left for me to carry. I watch my hat and coat, too.

Even if you cope successfully with those opening gambits, a second trial comes after the show. Unless you watch it, the projectors will be unplugged while they're sizzling hot. Then, still smoking, they are packed away in the case. Such treatment is hard on projector bulbs at fifteen dollars apiece. And if you think there are only a couple of ways to wrap up an extension cord, you should see the cat's-cradles that go into that back seat. I try to head off such difficulties by getting the burliest H.H. available to stand guard until things have calmed down and cooled off.

2. *The Eleventh-hour Engagement.* Maybe the plans weren't made yesterday, but under terms of the eleventh-hour engagement they might as well have been. Plenty of communication is necessary for a talk to go without a hitch: correspondence and telephone calls, posters and publicity, news coverage, to name a few. However, if some vital person along the line somehow remains unaware of your impending arrival, your whole visit may become a last-minute affair.

One time I was to give a talk in Green Bay, Wisconsin. The lady in charge of the program had done her job well. Her committee had put up posters and had arranged a couple of news interviews. The school where I was to speak had set aside the all-purpose room for the evening. She had even checked with other organizations to make sure there were no conflicting activities at the same time. Yet when I got there she was on the verge of tears.

"It's the custodian," she groaned. "He got sick yesterday. Nobody thought to tell his replacement about us. The school lunch tables are still set up. We'll need lots more chairs, and people are arriving already. What shall we do?"

Unaccustomed as I Am . . .   113

The sick man's replacement lived sixteen miles away, and would be of doubtful help anyway, so we decided not to call him. Instead, we began to fold the tables.

Those early arrivals, seeing what was happening, pitched in with us. Someone found the carts used to carry the tables and in a few minutes the tables were all wheeled away. As more people arrived, they joined us, began arranging chairs—and the talk started right on time.

Not only that, but there were plenty of willing hands to set the tables back in place after the show, too.

I just hope the custodian's union will understand in case one of their officials happens to read this account. Otherwise, I suppose some two hundred fifty residents of Green Bay and surrounding towns may find themselves picketed as unfair.

Another time I was the guest of Alice and Gordon Otis of Lexington Park, Maryland. We had set up the date five months previously, and were scheduled to use the gymnasium of a local school for the show. "What time would you like to go to the gym to set up your equipment?" Alice wanted to know.

"Oh, about six," I said.

She was taken aback. "Why so early, Ron? The show doesn't start until seven-thirty."

I could see what it was probably doing to her supper plans. However, I wanted to be doubly sure that everything was ready. Apologizing for rushing the meal, I told her that, since I had never seen the gymnasium, I wanted to take a look around. "To be sure there are no hidden complications," I said.

We had a hurry-up supper and got there at about six-fifteen. And, sure enough, there were complications. Not hidden ones, either—they were right in plain sight and all over the gymnasium. A basketball game was in progress.

"How was I supposed to know five months ago that we would be headed for the play-offs?" the assistant coach asked when I drew him aside. "Besides, this is just a scrimmage. We'll be through at seven."

So we enjoyed a basketball game instead of dessert that evening. It was an abbreviated game, though; the players were uneasy with us watching. The eleventh hour was approaching for them, too, and the final days of a winning season can make you forget everything else.

Yes, it always helps to get there ahead of time—especially if you're scheduled for a gymnasium in February.

Another early arrival on my part also produced unexpected results. I had been asked to speak at a little church in another part of my state. It was July and threatened to be a hot morning, so I decided to leave home early and enjoy a leisurely ride while it was cool. There was little traffic. Even driving slowly, I arrived well before ten for an eleven o'clock service.

Trying the door of the church, I found it unlocked. I went inside and sat down in a rear pew. Although the sun was bright outside, the church's interior was dim and peaceful. I slumped down a little, and closed my eyes.

A noise behind the altar jarred me awake. A door at that far corner of the church opened and a woman stepped in. She was clad only in a nightgown.

She glanced neither right nor left, but walked across the front of the church. Humming a little tune, she opened the door of a closet in the other corner. She took out a choir robe and put it on over her nightie. Then, seating herself at the organ, she began to practice her music.

So far, so good. Her secret would be safe with me. Indeed, I envied her scanty attire in the gathering July heat. But then I got to thinking, What if she looked up and saw me? She'd know I knew.

Slumping lower in the seat, I tried to figure a way out of it all. Then the organ stopped. Glancing up, I discovered that she had apparently dropped a sheet of music. While she was rummaging around on the floor I scuttled out the door. Then, when the music began again, I re-entered the church, wished her good morning, and sat down to enjoy the concert. Thoroughly.

Unaccustomed as I Am . . .   115

After the service I glanced around to see where she had come from. There were two or three houses close to the rear of the church, each screened from the others and from the road by a dense hedge. A quick dash from the front of one of them had been all that was needed. How she would get back to her house undetected, I didn't know. Perhaps she'd wear the choir robe home.

So, as I said, it pays to get there early. Even for a real eleventh-hour engagement. In this way there are no surprises. Or, if you're lucky, any surprise will be kept down to practically nothing at all.

3. *The Missing Microphone.* If the mike isn't actually missing, it's right there on the stage—but nobody knows how to run it. Allied to this is the mike that squeals. There's also the one that goes dead just as you start to speak.

First cousin to the M.M. is the Secret Switch. This, of course, controls the lights. Its whereabouts are known to a few select persons, none of whom are there. There's often a switch for the wall outlets, too—also a well-guarded secret. In a Grange hall near Rutland we made the interesting discovery that the wall outlets were geared to the house lights. Thus, every time the hall was darkened the projector died, too. Luckily someone in the audience recalled a procedure that had been used before. You ran the projector on a pair of hundred-foot extension cords from the yard light of a nearby house.

I've been in many an auditorium with impressive banks of levers so the main lights can be dimmed dramatically as you launch into your lecture—but the levers are all locked. Or, if they're unlocked, there's a formidable control box bearing the cryptic warning BE SURE TO FOLLOW OPERATING PROCEDURE.

Of course, someone is supposed to be there who knows about such things. But if it's an evening talk, say, there's some unflinching law that times your arrival exactly between the departure of the Day Man and advent of the Night Man. Hence, for all your good intentions in arriving well ahead of time, you discover something about early birds: they are also lonely.

Even if mike and lights are under control you're not out of it yet. There are other things that can go wrong, all the way through the talk. A bulb burns out. A latecomer produces an intriguing silhouette on the screen all the way down the center aisle. Somebody trips over an extension cord.

There's little protection against such unpredictables, I have discovered. A few quick jokes may help, but your heart is not in them. The audience scarcely listens, either. That extinct projector bulb has become the most important object in the world.

4. *The Timely Tot.* This youngster is familiar to us all. Just as you launch into something important, the Timely Tot tunes up. You finish your joke or your tale of high drama to the accompaniment of mentionable and unmentionable sounds

of malcontent. At last you feel like asking if there's a baby-sitter in the house.

One time a lady and a toddler sat down next to Peg just as the show began. The youngster climbed into Peg's lap and snuggled down, apparently for the rest of the evening. Peg smiled at the woman, who smiled back.

Things were fine for about ten minutes; then the child became restless. Not wanting to spoil the woman's enjoyment of the show, Peg held him as long as she could. Finally he became noisy, then downright obstreperous. So she hoisted him off her lap and tried to give him back. But the lady shrugged her shoulders and spread her hands helplessly. "What'll *I* do with him?" she whispered. "He's not mine!"

So Peg, my trusted Gal Friday, spent the rest of the evening walking the halls with somebody else's offspring. Luckily the visual equipment performed flawlessly, so I never knew she was gone. Later I commented about the woman who'd finally taken that screaming child out of the room.

"I wonder who that was?" I said, as much to myself as to Peg.

"Who was it?" echoed my long-suffering wife, shifting an extension cord to the other hand so she could carry the projector, too. "That, Sweetie, was me!"

5. *The Mechanical Marvel.* You're familiar with this bit of gadgetry, too. It may take many shapes and sizes and sounds. For example, if you're in a lecture room with the windows open on a summer day, the marvel roars to life on the lawn a few feet away. Or if, through some oversight, the lawn remains shaggy until you have departed, something else tunes up.

The air conditioner develops a rattle, perhaps. The fluorescent light hums a tune. The jackhammer crew rises from its coffee break. Today is vacuum-cleaner day in the lobby just outside the door. The Fire Department goes by.

These and other devices add variety to your talk. Someone sees that they are silenced, perhaps, or at least alleviated by closing doors and shutting windows. However, the damage is done. You've been distracted, if only momentarily, and while the meeting goes on apparently as before, you cannot erase that nagging little question back in your mind: "Where's the fire?"

6. *The Listless Listener.* You've already met her. Or him, or them. In fact, like me, you have been one yourself. If you don't think one dreamer cannot spoil your masterpiece of exposition with a single unguarded snore, you've got a lot to learn. And, speaking from experience, I hope you never learn it.

Time was when you could spot the L.L. by that vacant expression. Now, however, with two and one-half persons out of ten wearing sunglasses day and night there's an element of uncertainty among the audience. Those glasses that darken in bright light and sometimes remain hazy indoors do not help much, either. Together they screen off much of what is going on behind them. That is if there's anything going on at all.

Like the battlefield general, I have discovered that the best defense in such times is a good offense. Keep 'em guessing, if you can. That missionary's wildly waving sword did the trick, for instance. As one interested in animals, I have my own little advantage: I often take one of my small friends along.

Sparky, the gray squirrel, was such an addition to my talks. He accompanied me on more than two dozen lectures. He'd start the evening sedately enough, perched there on my shoulder, until the spirit of exploration hit him. Then he'd dash off into the audience. And, of course, he never got lost no matter how great the sea of humanity upon which he launched himself: the squirrel was in the center of the commotion.

One of Sparky's tricks involved an oversupply of sunflower seed. If you held out a handful of the seeds, he'd sit on your palm and shell them rapidly until he was full. Then, if there were still some seeds left, he'd fill his mouth and look for a spot to put them. Spying your shirt pocket, he'd quickly dump the mouthful there and turn back for more. While he was busy you could take the seeds out of the pocket, put them back in your hand—and he'd pick them up again. Back into your pocket, out again, back again. Over and over with the same seeds, until you tired of the game.

On a trip to a girl scout camp I gave each of the campers a few seeds. They held them out in their open hands near mine, and Sparky helped himself. Then he jumped back to me to store the extras in my shirt pocket as usual.

As it happened, I had a shirt with no pocket. This did not phase the little rodent, however. Squirrels are resourceful critters, and he solved the problem at once. He merely jumped over to the girl scout leader with his mouthful of seeds—and dumped them all down the front of her dress.

A much quieter pace was set by Piney, the porcupine who shared our home and hearts for a year. Friendly as a pup, he'd willingly climb from one person to another, murmuring in a little singsong voice and astounding people who found that a porcupine was not only personable but pettable.

Aided by animals which willingly carried on when I left off, I have been able to keep most Listless Listeners at bay. They are potentially at every lecture and slide talk, though, as are the rest of the perpetrators of Ronald's Rules of Disorder. It's a challenge to head them off, so to speak, before they ever get started.

One day, if I'm lucky, I may be in line again for a paean of praise such as was sounded by a youthful well-wisher after a show: "You know, Mr. Rood, this is the first time I've ever seen Uncle Arthur stay awake!"

There's one other old trouper I'd like to have you meet. We found her huddled in the center of the eastbound lane of Interstate 35 near Ottawa, Kansas. She was a Western painted turtle, doubtless out to find a place to lay a batch of eggs but completely nonplussed by the stream of traffic. Just as she'd work up enough nerve to proceed further, another car would roar overhead. Hastily pulling head and legs back into her shell, she'd wait for another break in traffic.

Obviously she'd be a goner if we didn't help. So I screeched the car to a halt, ran over and scooped her up, and continued on our way.

She was a pretty little creature. Olive green on her back, she was canary yellow underneath. A geometric pattern of brownish-gray occupied the center of her lower shell, while her legs were striped with red and black; green, yellow and red lines ran along her face and neck. Her personality matched her pleasing appearance, too: she was friendly from the start.

Alice, as we called her after the distaff segment of the team of Bill and Alice Myers with whom we stayed at Ottawa, was an ideal traveling companion. About as big around as a hamburger roll—but less portly—she sloshed about in a dishpan of water all the way from Kansas to Vermont. Her daily food supply was easily found. We'd pull off the road, overturn a log or old tin can, and extract an earthworm before it could escape. Dropping it in with Alice, we'd be on our way in a couple of minutes. Alice efficiently did the rest.

Such an attractive addition to our family deserved more than local recognition, I figured. So, on occasions where I'd be

Unaccustomed as I Am . . . 121

slated for a television appearance, I took Alice along. Slipping her into a pocket if I was pressed for space, or into a gallon plastic pail if I wasn't, I spirited my small reptilian friend aboard buses and taxis and planes for half a year. Then, when the time came for us to face the cameras, I had little to say or do. Alice stole the show.

She nearly got me in trouble with the authorities, too. There's a tiny airline that serves the city of Burlington, Vermont, supplementing the few jets that can sidle in through the Green Mountains daily and land at the airport's single major runway. It was on one of the aircraft of this small fleet that Alice and I came close to a brush with the law.

I had been on a junket to Cleveland and Pittsburgh. Alice had behaved beautifully all the way, except for a brief period of sulking at having to spend the night in a hotel washbasin. Everything went fine on the way back, too, until the last leg of my trip. Then I got aboard that commuter plane.

The commuter was a small twin-prop plane that held fifteen passengers. Setting Alice down in her plastic bucket, I took the cover off the bucket so she'd have plenty of air—and promptly forgot all about her. The next thing I knew there was a commotion up in the pilot's cabin. Then he stuck his head back and spoke to the passengers:

"Whose turtle is this?"

I looked quickly in the pail. No Alice. "Uh—I think it's mine."

"*Yours!* How'd you ever get it through the security gates?"

"Nothing insecure about a turtle. No metal, no explosives; she's just as friendly as can be."

Silence. Then, "You're sure you didn't let her go just so she could come up here to the cabin? And maybe disrupt the flight?"

"Hardly. Turtles don't follow instructions that well."

More silence. From the pilot and co-pilot, that is. The passengers were enjoying it immensely. Then another puzzled look. "What are you doing with a turtle on an airplane, any-way?"

"Well, you'll never believe it if I tell you, but she was on television this morning."

So I explained how I took her around with me and had had her on the "Marie Torre Show" in Pittsburgh, plus the "Morning Exchange" in Cleveland. The pilots grew wide-eyed, but still a bit suspicious. "Well," the co-pilot finally said, "you can have her back when you get to Burlington. For now we'll keep her up here."

"Do you want the bucket to keep her in?"

"No bucket. We've just got room for a turtle."

So I took my seat again, to the accompaniment of thought-ful stares from the fourteen other passengers. Obviously they had been impressed with the proceedings.

When we finally got to Burlington the pilot handed me the turtle. By this time, an hour after they had discovered her, they had become quite well acquainted. "Alice, did you enjoy the trip?" I asked.

"She sure did," the pilot grinned at me. "If we'd had another couple of hours, she'd have learned to fly. But she seemed a little air sick."

"Yep," the co-pilot added. "Her color wasn't too good. But she's okay now."

So I returned Alice to her bucket, thanked them for her care, and took her to Peg and our waiting car.

Many times, of course, I have had to put in an appearance without any animals to help keep the conversation moving. Once I wanted to take my quarter-wolf, Laska (the other three-quarters is Siberian husky), for a Boston appearance. When I proposed to bring on eighty-five pounds of pooch for her first television show, however, the show's manager balked.

"Tame parrots, yes," she said. "Performing dogs, goldfish, even chimpanzees. But no wolves."

So Laska got her television at second hand from in front of the tube in our living room in Vermont. Peg says Laska was unimpressed; didn't even recognize the sound of my voice.

Early in my TV career I was scheduled for a show that would be taped on the West Coast. It was to be my first national appearance. The show was in connection with a book I had written titled *Animals Nobody Loves*. A supplier out on the coast was to provide half a dozen unloved critters for the appearance: a turkey vulture, wolf, snake and warthog, among others. We were to talk about each one in turn while the camera zoomed in for a close-up.

I boarded the plane and winged my way to California. Recalling other occasions when I had welcomed plenty of extra time, I appeared at the studios half a day early. Chatting with the manager of the show, I was relieved to learn that the animals had but a few miles to travel. "They should arrive before six," the manager assured me.

Maybe they *should* arrive before six, but they didn't. The

RONALD ROOD

day was oppressively hot. Half the state of California was trying to escape to the beaches, and the animals got caught in a
traffic snarl. The audience was already seated in the studio
when the truck pulled into the parking lot.

I had planned to make at least a brief acquaintance with each
animal. I had also wanted to have a chat with their trainer so
I'd have a little background of familiarity. Now, however,
there was no time.

And no trainer. That little detail was left to me. If you have
read Shakespeare's *Comedy of Errors* you know how one mistake can pile on another. Such was the case here. The man
who brought the cages into the studio was merely the driver.
His task was to deliver the animals and take them home safely
after the show. "Plus get the insurance papers signed," he
added.

The manager whirled to face him. "What insurance papers?"

"The ones I'm supposed to get signed before the animals go
on the show. These are valuable critters and something could
happen to them."

At this the manager bridled. " 'Something could happen to
them'?" he exploded. "What about us? Who's going to be responsible if somebody gets chewed?"

Four minutes to air time. And there they stood, glaring at
each other. Something had to give—and right away. "Oh,
that's all right," I said breezily, "we can do a show without
animals. I've done it dozens of times—"

Now the manager turned on me. "Not here you haven't.
No animals, no act. No act, no show. It's off."

I was incredulous. "*Off?*"

But he had made up his mind. Hastening to the wings of
the stage he announced the change in plan. The curtains
parted, the audience cheered and the show was on.

Numbly, I watched the whole thing on one of the back-
stage monitors. I heard the animals being taken back to the
truck. Just a few feet away the patter went on, with minute

Unaccustomed as I Am . . .

after precious minute draining away. The talk was all about animals, yes—but I wasn't there.

Then the show was over.

In the movies I'd have rushed on stage, captured the crowd in an instant, and become a national star. But this wasn't the movies, with a chance to study the script. This was a horrendous dream in real life. By the time I'd realized that it was all actually happening, the psychological moment for a bombshell appearance had passed.

It was one of the most frustrating experiences I've ever had.

Luckily, another national show involving the same book turned out quite the other way. It was Garry Moore's popular show, "To Tell the Truth," and it was fun from the start.

Away I went once more. I was determined to be ready for 'em if something should go wrong, but it went without a hitch. Not one hint of Ronald's Rules of Disorder was to be found.

In case you're not familiar with "To Tell the Truth," this is the show where a guest and two impostors appear before a panel. With Garry Moore as master of ceremonies to help call the shots, the four members of the panel ask as many questions about the topic at hand as is possible in the allotted time. They may address their queries to any of the three contestants they choose. The two impostors are free to answer any way they like, but the real guest must tell the truth.

The panel members make their guesses. Then, in a dramatic scene of enlightenment, Garry Moore says, "Will the real Whatzisname please stand up!"

There's a shuffling of feet, a suspenseful moment, and Whatzisname—who may not have been the one you thought at all—rises to be revealed.

I met my two impostors the day before the show. Discovering that all three of us liked to walk, we spent the afternoon hiking most of the way up one side of Broadway and back down the other, cramming for tomorrow's exam. I told them the questions that had been asked me most often about those unloved animals: what good is a mosquito, for instance, and has a wolf ever attacked a human being?

Sure enough, those questions came up on the show. One of the impostors answered correctly, saying that no wolf or wolf pack has ever made an unprovoked attack on a human being—adding, helpfully, that "wolves are so terrible that if one ever did attack, you'd never live to tell about it anyway." The other, rather than saying mosquitoes were valuable food for dozens of species of birds and little fish, launched into a straight-faced tirade that covered nearly everything from space shots to a cure for warts.

The impostors had done their work well. Only Jack Cassidy of the four panelists guessed right. Happy that I'd been able to redeem myself a bit after that other débâcle, I said farewell to my two cronies. Later, as I relaxed on the plane, I told myself it was great to be on a national show where people didn't know who you were—and even greater to be going to my little town where they *did* know.

I stopped at a gas station in Bristol on the way home from the airport. Word had traveled of my visit to the Big City, and the lad at the pumps was all questions.

"Say, Ron, I hear you was on TV the other day."

"Yep." (Modestly.)

"One of them quiz shows?"

"Right. 'To Tell the Truth.' "

"Is that where they say, 'Will the real Somebody please stand up?' "

"That's the one, Charley."

"Oh. And who were *you* supposed to be?"

Yessir. I was home, all right. And it was delightful.

One last little story before I close this chapter. It concerns one of the most joyous interviews I've had, and gives a little insight into the methods of a topnotch interviewer. My hostess, known to millions of radio listeners over the years in an appreciative circle around New York City was that warm and gracious lady, Martha Dean.

Unaccustomed as I Am . . .   127

I was ushered into a room at Radio WOR just a few seconds before another door opened and a slim woman stepped in. "I'm Martha Dean," she said. "And you are the man who wrote this book."

She placed a copy of *Animals Nobody Loves,* the book we were to discuss, on the table before her. I looked at it in surprise. Although the publisher had sent it to her less than a month previously it looked as if it had come from a lending library. It had obviously been opened again and again. The dust jacket had been removed and there were six or eight strips of paper marking special pages. She knew nearly as much about the book as I did.

"I enjoyed the book," she said. Then she indicated two sets of notes. "One of these interviews concerns how important it is to maintain good environmental conditions so that wildlife and plants will have a chance. The other interview deals with the fun of learning and talking about animals. Which interview would you rather have?"

I figured people got enough, day after day after day, about our environment and how to preserve it. "Let's talk about the fun of animals," I said.

With a sweeping gesture, she flung one set of notes clear across the room. When she turned back, her face was wreathed in smiles. "Correction," she said. "I *loved* the book. Now we'll both have fun!"

And fun we did have, indeed. We laughed and joked all the way through an astonishingly short half hour.

In fact, it has all been fun, over the years. Two decades have passed since those hesitant scouters showed up at my front door. But if they should read these words, I hope they'll let me know who they are. I sure owe them a lot.

7. *A Sense of Wonder*

Peg and I love to share our experiences with school children. She accompanies me on my talks when she can; it's a sort of busman's holiday from her kindergarten job. Most of the time, however, I go alone. She's still with me in a way, just the same: many of the experiences I tell the kids about have been those my wife and I have had together. There was the time, for instance, when we were guests in the home of Madame Pele.

Madame Pele is a torrid bombshell. She lives deep within the volcanic pits of Hawaii, her eyes flashing and her long hair flowing as she tosses her head in anger. She bears a constant quarrel with the upper world.

Every few months, she has had enough. Gathering herself,

she explodes in rage. Billows of sulfurous smoke pour out her door. The earth trembles and shakes. Sparks shoot into the air. Ashes, cinders and rocks roar skyward, falling back as a deadly rain.

Then comes the lava. Flowing from a tortured gash in the mountain's side, or perhaps bubbling higher within its bowels until it spills over the volcano's rim, the molten stream advances over the countryside. It consumes everything in its path. Even rain-soaked trees burst into flame at the first touch. Sometimes the lava races like a demonic river; other times it inches along slowly in a blackened, crumbling wall.

Those terrible tantrums of Pele are frightening to behold. Nevertheless, with modern instruments one can predict when she is about to vent her rage. The swelling of the mountain can be measured, like that of a bubble of oatmeal before it bursts. Earth tremors, carefully gauged, reveal how much the rocks have shifted beneath the ground. Listening devices tell of the pressure and flow of subterranean rivers of fiery magma, a thousand times more viscous than water.

Long ago the angry volcano goddess was appeased with human sacrifice. In more enlightened times, cranberry-like opelo berries have been tossed into the pit—no mean feat, either, in the face of that scorching heat and the deadly, smothering fumes. Today, although the goddess still storms and rages, her mortal neighbors endure her wrath. Her anger will subside, as it has before.

We had been fortunate to be visiting my brother Jim and his family in Hilo during one of Pele's outbursts. Realizing how great it would be to share her story with school children back home, we ventured to the rim of the crater. Standing at the edge of the visitors' platform, we took pictures of that fiery caldera below us. We gathered a few pieces of lava, plus a fire-blackened twig that had miraculously escaped being consumed.

Back in New England, I assembled my slides and souvenirs into a talk on forces that shape the earth. Although a couple

RONALD ROOD

of trips to Hawaii scarcely made me an authority, I was able to make a story of what I had seen.

One visit to a second grade will long remain in my memory. I had shown my best slides of the inferno. Where the lava flowed to the ocean, a great pillar of steam, rising a mile into the air, could almost be heard to roar as the molten rock poured into the sea, adding an acre a day to the coastline of Hawaii. Then, turning off the projector, I passed around a chunk of lava, a few pieces of volcanic ash, and that charred bit of wood.

After we had talked a bit about the searing heat, the choking smoke, and the skies that glowed at night, I asked the students to bring the materials to the front of the room. One student brought the wood, another the volcanic ash. A youngster came forward with the lava, his eyes wide. "Mr. Rood," he said, carefully cradling that material that had been through two dozen hands before it got to him, "it's still warm!"

It is moments like that which make me realize the tremendous power—and the awful responsibility—that is vested in those who shape the minds of children. To be able to make a lump of lava come to life, so to speak, or to have a child come up to you in tears after you've let the class pet your great horned owl because "my brother and I shot an owl last winter, and now I wish I'd shot myself, Mr. Rood!"—that is all the success I need. Something of what I feel has struck a chord in a young life. What greater reward could there be?

One time I was a guest at a small elementary school. The teacher and students of a certain class had been reading a book of mine, and a student had written on her own to invite me to pay a visit. So, the next time I knew my travels would take me in that direction, I dropped her a note saying I'd be there.

When I arrived, youthful Anne was called from class to escort me around. She showed me the tiny gymnasium, the cafeteria, the glass case in the front hall that prominently displayed two of my books. She took me to the library where there was a whole bulletin board embarrassingly full of dust jackets from others of my books, plus newspaper clippings and a couple of my articles in *Ranger Rick's Nature Magazine.*

It all gave me a warm feeling, yes. In a little school in a small town my visit could well have been greater than the inauguration of a President and the first step on the moon combined. My small friend Anne doubtless gained a new stature, too—one that she might remember for years to come. To be the perpetrator of such an event is, indeed, an accomplishment.

But, as I said, it's likewise a responsibility. The school invited me to be its guest at the noon lunch. As I stood in the cafeteria line, boys and girls walked by with food, trays, bottles of milk, napkins. And almost all of them brushed me lightly as they went past. It was their youthful, bashful, completely wonderful way of greeting. I just hoped I was somehow worthy of their confidence.

Peg is familiar with this "importance of the physical," as she calls it, in her kindergarten classes. "When they sit quietly while I read them a story," she says, "I feel I have their attention. But when they press against me so hard that sometimes I cannot turn the pages, I know I have their love."

Back in the dim past, in the benighted era before the advent of those items of clothing known as pantyhose, women often wore garter belts to hold up their stockings. It was on one of those early days that Peg got the feeling she had "arrived" as a teacher. "I was standing on the playground, discussing something with another teacher," she recalled that evening. "There were kids all around—some running, some swinging on the swings, and three or four standing quietly next to us as we talked. Then I realized what my little Mark and my little Julie were doing. One was at my left side, one at my right—absentmindedly tracing the bumps of the fasteners of my garter belt with their fingers as they stood and absorbed every word we were saying."

This touch-see-smell world of childhood can be simple and direct. "Don't try to be fancy with your Christmas presents," Peg told her kindergarten class one December day. "Just give your friends what you think they'd really like."

Her words came back to her sooner than she expected. The day before vacation many of the children brought gifts for the teacher. One package, about the size of a flashlight, was laboriously done up in scotch tape—obviously wrapped by the youthful giver himself.

Inside the package? A can of deodorant.

Peg used to con me into visiting her school a couple of times a year. This was a fringe benefit, I suppose, of being married to a teacher. Since my family had raised turkeys when I was young, as a former real, live turkey-raiser I went along with her class to Kneeshaw's turkey farm the week before Thanksgiving. I was supposed to help her keep an eye on a busload of kids.

The children surveyed several acres of range populated by the great birds. They gobbled back at the gobblers in the open yards, and heard a most enlightening talk by one of the farm workers. They saw a turkey egg, learned how much grain it took to raise a single bird, and were given a couple of feathers each to take home.

It was a rewarding visit, and the children enjoyed it hugely. The main point, however, may have eluded them in spite of it all. "What Mary and I want to know," said a little girl when we asked if they had any final questions, "is—how does the meat get inside the turkey?"

Once we took the class to Bob Douglas's orchard. The youngsters watched the boxes of apples being brought into

the packing house where the fruit was sorted and put up for shipment. Each munching an apple, the kindergarteners then trouped to the cider mill, where they watched as the apples were washed, pulped, and pressed into cider. Then Bob took them out to the orchard where several pickers were busy among the trees. "Now," he said, "I want you to go and help yourself to some apples right off the tree."

"But how will we know which apples to pick?" asked one little boy.

"Oh, they'll tell you," Bob answered.

At this the youngster was dumfounded. "Apples can't talk!" he said.

It's this disarming directness—both in listening and speaking —that makes it such a joy to talk to youngsters.

It's fun to get their letters, too. Sandy McClellan of South Burlington, for instance, wrote me because "we are doing a report on famish people of Vermont." A youthful friend whom I had known for several years laid it on the line with this: "Our teacher says we should write to someone important and if not someone important someone interesting and I thought of you. Do you know anybody?"

Seldom do I make a school visit without gaining some refreshing new glimpse of the world as seen through youthful eyes. "One of my ears can't listen," partially-deaf David confided as he took his place in the front row at one of my talks. Small Michael, happy with my color slides of animals, wondered "when are we having another film festival?" And when I thanked Brian for his gift of what I thought was a picture of a cow, he put me in my place. "If it was a cow," he said reprovingly, "it would have tips."

One school year I put together a traveling zoo composed of a sleepy but impressive boa constrictor, a skunk, a raccoon and a turtle. My motorized menagerie resulted in a flurry of letters. I'd like to share a few of them with you.

"Dear Mr. Rood [wrote one boy]. Thank you for coming

to our school. This is the first time I ever had a five foot snack around my neck. I hope I can do it again. Your Friend, Daniel."

Another had a way with words:

"I thought you knew a lot about animals. I still think so. Your wild life is very interesting."

One boy refused to let his spelling interfere with his enjoyment of the program. In a burst of enthusiasm he wrote, "My friends and I have all desided on a word for your talk. And that word is grate."

Then there was an unadorned comment from a small girl with interesting powers of observation. "The turtle," she said accusingly, "went to the bathroom behind the desk."

One youngster let me know how he felt about it all when he wrote, "Thank you for coming to visit our school. I hope I can see you aging." Another, apparently unable to wait that long, asked me to "please write to me if you have time. If you do not have time, please write when you do."

I trust it was a tight schedule that occasioned this lad's letter:

"After your talk I got your book about How Do You Spank a Porcupine. I have read 39 pages so far. I don't know if I will read any more."

Time apparently collapsed on one fifth-grader. She was just able to compose the following: "Dear Mr. Rood. How are you? Well I have to go now. Please write back. Your friend, Darlene."

A Sense of Wonder   135

One small correspondent informed me that "my teacher says we have to write and thank you for coming. Thank you." Another said, "I want to tell you that I am sorry for saying my father shot the hawk because you love animals so much." A New Jersey boy petted a woodchuck at one of my talks and then conjured up an interesting scene in a letter a few days later. "A woodchuck," he wrote, "was running around the field in a mysterious way. Finally I found out why. My German Shepard was chasing him."

Other bits of information I have gleaned from letters include the observation that "the lava you gave us will not float because Marty Harrington and I put it in the water," plus the welcome news that "before your talk I didn't like snakes. Now I am not so sure." After I'd given a talk about how some birds depend on others to raise their young, an eighth-grader concluded that "I think it is shameful that the cuckoo does not lay its own eggs." One of her classmates volunteered that "we saw a bat just like yours on the porch but we left it alone because it might be rapid."

The enthusiasm of those youngsters is fun enough when they're in a classroom. Take them outside and the pleasure is doubled. The lower grades are already interested, with the natural curiosity about the world that is normal to youth. As soon as you suggest it, they readily touch and feel and smell

RONALD ROOD

and taste a fuzzy plant or a fluffy seedpod. They solemnly survey a hole in the ground and have a great time guessing what might have made it.

Interesting facts about plants and animals become painless memory aids: the way butter-and-eggs yawns when you squeeze it, for instance, or the galloping gait of a squirrel that results in its hind feet landing in front of its forefeet so the tracks seem as if it was running backwards.

Even worldly high school students, those who have been everywhere and seen everything, may find there are yet a few crannies around the school building or a vacant lot that hold a secret or two. It's a challenge to help such students look for those secrets—and a delight when they begin searching on their own.

That ash tree in the school yard, for instance: it's the parent of Bill's hockey stick, Hal's baseball bat and Judy's tennis racket. The blue chicory by the No PARKING sign makes a good substitute for coffee. The berries on the juniper growing by the front entrance could be used in the flavoring of certain drinks, hard and soft, from soda pop to gin. Those aphids on the bush are related to the lac insect from which we get shellac—and nearly every teenage car and cycle buff knows about shellac.

In July and August I often have the chance to visit summer camps. Here, surrounded by the outdoors on all sides, boys and girls learn how interesting and important the woods and fields and water can be. With guidance they can collect a meal of edible plants. They become old friends with trees that supply them with necessities, including the syrup on their pancakes and the hard wooden lane of a bowling alley. The night sounds lose their terror as a youngster counts a cricket's chirps, makes a calculation, and triumphantly announces the temperature. An animal track, a broken twig, a colorful flower —each may have a story to tell.

One July day I was a guest at Ken Webb's Farm and Wilderness Camp in Plymouth, Vermont. "The nature trail starts off by the edge of the garden," Ken said, with a wave of his hand. "The kids'll show you where it goes from there. Hope you find plenty to talk about with them along the way."

I started out with a dozen campers. Aided by their sharp eyes and keen senses I did, indeed, find "plenty to talk about." We discovered the hollow-tree home of a litter of flying squirrels. We solemnly contemplated the shelving ledge that served as a chipmunk's front door. We found a "nest" the size of a bathtub where a deer had bedded down. We made balloons from the thick leaves of the succulent plant known as live-forever, and carved whistles out of the twigs of a willow.

An hour later we returned to the garden. There a second dozen campers was waiting. We covered the same ground as the first group, and found nearly as many new items as before. The third dozen, fully as curious as the rest, helped discover still more of interest along the same route.

At lunch Ken and I were talking about the morning's walks. After I'd told him about the wildlife, plants and insects we had met along the way, he asked if I had any suggestions for improvement of the trail.

"Not really," I told him. "Nature has landscaped it pretty well. There's plenty to interest those kids at every step. The only thing I might add is to have it go in a loop so you don't have to backtrack to get home again."

"But it *is* in a loop, Ron."

"Really? How big a loop?"

"Small. Not even half a mile."

Of course. Those campers had become so enthused with what they found along the trail that they'd stopped me at almost every step. Every time we'd get going someone would say, "What's this?" and we'd pause again.

Three hours spent on about five hundred yards of woodland path and we'd never even gotten into high gear. That's what a bunch of kids can do when something catches their fancy.

It reminded me of a comment once made by Louis Agassiz, who was asked what he had done during the summer. "Oh," said the renowned naturalist, "I spent it traveling. I got half-way across my yard."

The sense of wonder can do amazing things to your perspective. The poet John Frederick Nims was taking his leisure on the rolling campus of the Bread Loaf Writers' Conference in Vermont one August day. A mile or so away the rocks and cliffs piled on each other to form the spine of the Green Mountains. One conferee, who had never been in hilly country before, looked at a distant peak as she talked with Nims.

"Is that a mountain?" she asked.

"Yes," he agreed, "it is."

"Golly," she said, "there ought to be a bigger word for it!"

That girl's spontaneous outburst is echoed nearly every time someone's eyes are opened to the world around us. "I could sit and look at that mountainside all day," said a boy fresh from the city, as we paused and contemplated the cloud shadows moving across the face of a steep slope. "You never see cloud pictures where it's flat. Only clouds—if the air is clear enough."

One of my personal joys is to help people get over their fears and prejudices regarding animals. It's amazing what changes can be wrought if a person can meet a supposedly fearsome critter face to face in an atmosphere of mutual good will. When we had our small porcupine it was fun to encourage people to pet him before we'd tell them what he was. Many people are familiar with pictures of porkies with their quills erected and ready for business. Few, however, have seen one with those wicked spears at rest and hidden beneath the outer coat of hair. Thus they'd have little inkling of the potential of the creature they were handling so casually.

Then, right in mid-pet, so to speak, I'd reveal Piney's identity. There'd be a pause—a sort of catching of breath, I suppose—and you could just see the new interest that shone in the person's eyes. Often it would seem to be little short of a revelation. "A porcupine!" they'd say, stroking him anew, "well, I'll be darned!"

Once when visiting a school near Omaha, I was scheduled

to give a talk on snakes. The class, I discovered, had just that morning received a four-foot boa constrictor from a co-operative unit that loaned animals to area schools. Warm, well-fed and comfortable, Julius Squeezer was still in his shipping cage. The teacher to whose care he was entrusted told me that Julius had thousands of friends in the Omaha area. He had graced the necks of hundreds of impromptu snake-charmers in classrooms of more than two dozen schools.

Could I borrow him for my talk? "Sure, Ron. He'd be delighted. Just don't forget to give him plenty of love."

So I talked about snakes, showing a couple of small specimens of my own and using Julius Squeezer as the grand finale. " 'Just don't forget to give him plenty of love,' " I repeated to the students as they passed him around among them. So, dutifully, they told him how beautiful and smooth he was, and how much they loved him.

When the show was over and the boa was back in his cage, I asked the students what they thought about snakes now. They told how shiny he was, how he pressed back when he was stroked, how bright his colors—but nothing about what he *wasn't:* cold, clammy, creepy and all the other things people imagine about snakes.

It remained for one small girl to put words to what happens when your prejudices come face to face with the facts. "I can't really tell about snakes," she said, "because Julius isn't an ordinary one. He's— Well, he's Julius!"

Perhaps that's the key: recognize the personality of a critter and you lose much of your dread. I can think of storybook and cartoon animals who have become almost human because they've acquired a name and a real or imagined personality.

Of course a fictitious mouse named Mickey is still worlds removed from that furtive creature in the garbage or out by the rubbish heap, but Mickey is at least a start. The real-life Smokey may have helped people to understand bears—or at least the problems they face. And the genuine Rascal isn't just any raccoon—he's one certain individual. But the fortunate few who have met Smokey or Rascal will never again view all bears or all raccoons as alien, forbidding wild animals.

This was the way it turned out with Barney, a baby woodchuck. We found him, slightly injured, on a busy roadway. Too dazed to get out of the way, he huddled on the pavement while cars and trucks straddled his crouching form. I rescued him, took him home, treated his skinned nose, and discovered that he was completely given to us from that moment onward. His friendliness knew no bounds. He'd snuggle in your arms for an hour, if you sat still that long.

As in many rural areas, in Vermont the woodchuck is looked on with disfavor. About the only redeeming feature it's supposed to have is that annual pilgrimage to the upper world from its winter burrow. Then, as the famous groundhog, it utters its prognostications on the second of February. The rest of the time it spends digging 'chuck holes to break the legs of incautious cows and the axles of unwary tractors.

Small matter that those holes may be used by more than a dozen other mammals to raise their young. It means little, either, that they're welcome refuges for any creatures to escape a diving hawk or a racing grass fire, or that the tunnels aerate and irrigate the soil. The only good 'chuck, say most of my neighbors as they shoulder their varmint rifles, is a dead one.

Thus we were glad when a youngster could take time out to meet Barney. Those agile front paws, the human-looking ears, the contented murmur as ten pounds of fur settles down

into your lap: no wild woodchuck would seem quite the same once you'd met its not-so-wild cousin.

I could sense the change in attitude in the breathless grimaces of small potential "varminteers" as the portly little creature stood up in a lap, put trusting paws on a chest, and nuzzled at a chin in the rodent version of "I like you!" In fact, one youngster made it all official:

"We will still get rid of starlins [she wrote] and Jimmy and me still dont like porkupines, but every time I see a groundhog I think of Barny and how he ate my cracker."

How long will her change of heart last? It's hard to say. The farmer has to live in Vermont, too, even though the groundhog was here first. But at least with one little girl the peaceful rodent has had its day in court. She has seen both sides.

Indeed, that's one of the most rewarding results of my visits to schools and camps and youth groups. I can help children and those who guide them to take a fresh look at what they may have lost: the sense of wonder at the lives of their wild neighbors.

One of my more improbable accomplices in such an effort has been a small creature by the name of Lucy. This little lady weighs scarcely a pound. Her nearsighted eyes blink a welcome in your direction and her whiskers tickle as she brushes your skin in greeting. Give her a kernel of corn and she'll sit up, holding it in two tiny hand-like paws as if it was an entire ear. Lucy is—brace yourself—a common brown rat.

No. An uncommon brown rat. She was born in captivity and has known nothing but human kindness all her life. She is the ward of Carol Krieg, a friend of mine in the Zoology Department at the University of Vermont. Carol goes about her work in the laboratory half the time with Lucy companionably perched on her shoulder. The personable little critter is a born ham; she has been with Carol and me on television, and has accompanied us to several schools.

Small enough to nestle in a coat pocket or in Carol's handbag, Lucy is also able to crawl into a loose sleeve. Gifted with an outsized curiosity, she pokes around from wrist to elbow to shoulder, making intriguing lumps in the clothing of the delighted youngster. Then as a curtain call she'll peek out of the collar. Whiskers twinkling, she'll convulse the whole room.

During one of Lucy's visits a boy tried to pass her along to a classmate by holding his arm out so she could crawl onto his friend's shoulder. But Lucy hadn't finished exploring Boy Number One yet. No matter how he twisted and contorted, she went over and under, down and around with sure-footed ease. "Wow!" he gasped, when the transfer was finally made, "she's awful climby!"

Lucy the rat, Barney the 'chuck, Shadow the weasel, Piney the porcupine and half a dozen other critters over the years made friends in scores of classrooms. It is nice to have a return engagement at one of those schools and have some youngster stop me in the halls with "Mr. Rood, how's Lucy?"

Of course, it's nice to be remembered for yourself, too—not merely for the animals you have along. Thus you can imagine my pleasure on receiving a letter from a youthful fan after I had given a slide talk at a school in Bristol, Connecticut.

"Dear Mr. Rood, thank you for your talk and for signing my autograph book. I will tell you what I did when I got home for it is something I have never done before. I took your autograph right in and showed it to my stuffed dog, Snappy."

Other writers may count their ratings on book lists, their appearances on national television, the reviews they get in the Sunday papers. I enjoy such measures of success, too; it's good to know your books are being opened, here and there. But to have a file bulging with letters signed "your freind," and to find that you have been privileged to enter the secret world of a small girl and her favorite plaything—that is a warm feeling indeed.

8. *The Happy Equation*

Part of the fun of getting people and animals together is that you seldom know what'll happen. People react in different ways, and so do animals. They've given me many a chuckle—and a story—in the process.

Nor do birds and animals always have to meet us in person. Often a brush with our gadgetry is enough.

Witness the birds that went in for soap operas. I suppose the story could be called "As the Antenna Turns."

It began with Karen Webster and her afternoon shows. She'd watch one program, flip the selector, turn the rotor, and watch two more. When that antenna on her roof swung around from west to southeast, its rods ended up right where they'd get the heat from her chimney. The birds would fly up from her neighbor's feeder and perch in the outpouring warmth.

Often there'd be a spate of bickering until the hierarchy of the pecking order was established and each bird found its place. Such antics apparently jiggled some loose connection and gave Karen a picture that was all static and snow and wavy lines until things settled down. "I'm glad they do it at the beginning of the program," she told me. "Thank goodness for the commercial!"

Another bird that knew a good thing when it saw it was a short-legged, goggle-eyed, mottled brown creature the size of your fist. Known as a woodcock or timber-doodle, this land-going sandpiper makes its living largely by feeding on earthworms. Naturally, its wriggly prey is in short supply when the ground is frozen, and the woodcock must wing its way to warmer climes.

Things were different, however, for a woodcock at a ski resort near Stowe. One feature of the resort is a heated outdoor swimming pool. Guests can run through the icy blasts and plunge into the balmy waters, cavorting and splashing in zero weather. The overflow from such activity disappears into a drain. Traveling underground, it surfaces a discreet distance away where it is out of sight. Then it flows down the mountainside. The surrounding soil is warm and moist, with a fine crop of earthworms a few feet away from dead center, where the effect of the chlorine has lessened. And there, too, the resourceful woodcock plied its trade all one winter.

Probing the mud with its bill, the "bog sucker" extracted the earthworms necessary to its daily existence. It nearly broke up the local bird club on its Christmas count, too: a woodcock in *December*?

One bird opportunist on a Long Island estate outsmarted itself. A woman had put her parakeet out in its cage to get some sun on a balmy winter day. When she went to take it in later, the parakeet was gone. In its place was a northern shrike. This predatory bird, about the size of a robin, had beat its way in through the flimsy bars of the cage. The frantic parakeet managed to escape through the space, but the shrike was unable to force its way back out again.

Opportunity knocked—literally—for a certain woodpecker one spring day. Woodpeckers are scarcely gifted with much of a voice to charm the opposite sex; hence they proclaim their intentions by whacking on a resounding hollow stub. This, I suppose, is the counterpart of screeching tires and roaring mufflers among our own species.

This particular woodpecker apparently somehow concluded that if a little noise was good, ten times as much might be better. The sounding board for his declaration was our barn roof. A piece of the metal roofing had come loose in a storm and curled upward. There it stood: a ready-made microphone, amplifier and speaker, all in one. Several times a day during mating season, while lesser males tapped out an amorous Morse code on ordinary trees, that woodpecker boomed out his availability like an airborne jackhammer.

The gray dawn was the time the bird would choose for his first ear-splitting serenade. After several days of this, I figured he must have gotten his point across to the gentle sex, so I nailed the metal back in place. I never did find out if he won the choicest lady of them all with his tactics, but there's no accounting for taste, anyway. Which may be as true in the bird kingdom as in our own—and easier on the eardrums of both.

The little falcon known as the kestrel is also called a sparrow hawk because it is colored like many sparrows, not because it catches them. Its normal food consists of grasshoppers and other insects, plus an unlucky small rodent or frog. Yet the habits of an occasional kestrel have begun to change—and it's largely our fault.

Ordinarily the kestrel goes far enough south in winter to find some open ground over which to hunt its food. Now, however, there's a new bonanza right at home. In fact, the snowier the winter the better the pickings. At an estimated fifty million feeders in the United States and Canada, there's a

146   RONALD ROOD

tempting concentration of birds. One quick swoop—and the robin-sized raptor has its meal for the day.

Peg and I saw this happen at the feeder in our front yard. We had no sooner identified the rust-colored bird with the black-and-white facial markings than the newcomer left its perch. Dropping from the telephone pole where it had been sitting, it zoomed behind a spruce, banked around it in a power turn—and picked off a small bird before its prey had time to take wing.

As chance would have it, the victim had been an English sparrow—that blatant freeloader which muscles its way into bird feeders, bird baths and even bird houses whether they're already occupied or not. Thus we were not overly saddened to see it go. However, we figured the kestrel would be back, so we moved the feeder away from the screening spruce. The birds were more in the wind now, but they had a better chance to see the hawk coming.

We felt sorry for the kestrel. It had to earn a living, too. Besides, the presence of such predators helps keep other birds perky, bright and alert in their actions. So we were relieved to see that once it had sampled the offerings around our house it turned its attentions to the easy pickings around the barn. There it was able to snatch an occasional English sparrow that flew out from beneath the eaves. Thus, for the three weeks it stayed, the falcon brought a bit of poetic justice into the lives of those garrulous gate-crashers.

Opportunity can strike almost anywhere. Our daughter Janice carefully arranged and hung bunches of colorful dried Indian corn on the outside doors of her house for a Hallowe'en party. It was a party, all right—for the blue jays, which stripped each bunch of half its kernels before the first guest arrived.

My friend Bessie Pixley has one of the greenest vegetable gardens in Lincoln. She plants according to weather signs, and follows many methods used for centuries by the Indians. One proven way to get a bumper crop is to bury a fish head

beneath each hill of corn. The decaying flesh acts as fertilizer, and the corn flourishes mightily.

I was with Bessie one morning as she walked out for a look at the garden. Sure enough, you could tell without question which hills of corn had been favored with a piscatorial cocktail. Each one had been demolished. A passing raccoon had sniffed out the tasty morsels and there was nary a fish head left. Nary a corn plant, either.

A local fisherman told me how he acquired an unexpected friend just because the fishing was so poor. "I was sitting on the bank at the lake," he recalled, "and all I was getting was little sunfish. At first I threw them back, but they kept on coming. So I decided, Heck, they're better than nothing. There's no size or bag limit for them anyway, so I tossed each one behind me in the grass."

He had thrown three or four up on the bank when he heard a little noise. "When I looked back I saw a big old raccoon. He was just polishing off my latest fish. So I tossed him the next one I caught and he ate that one, too. Then he waited in the grass and grabbed each fish as I threw it to him."

148

A raccoon—almost any raccoon—can provide enough yarns to prove how resourceful a wild animal can be. I'll allow myself just one more 'coon story, however, as there are other creatures I'd like you to meet.

The story is about a raccoon that visited the garbage pail of a friend. At first everything was fine, but soon the animal got carried away in all that abundance. It began to scatter debris around the back yard. So my friend and his son put a heavy stone on the lid of the garbage pail. Too large for the raccoon to budge, the stone would put a stop to it all, they figured.

The next morning, though, the weight had been removed. The lid was off and the yard bore its customary morning-after look. So that night they replaced the stone and watched by the window to see how it was done.

And how *was* it done? Easily. The raccoon merely stood up and pushed against the garbage pail. The container, battered and misshapen, was scarcely flat-bottomed anyway, and it began to rock. A few more shoves and the stone tumbled off.

Not that the raccoon had figured this all out, of course. It had just leaned against the barrel as usual and found that it swayed ponderously under the touch. Then, because raccoons will often move anything that'll wiggle, it happened on the right solution.

So much for raccoons. But I cannot resist one parting shot. It has to do with the habit these little burglars have of traveling around in a family group, sort of like a troupe of clowns. Usually this results in mutual protection, but on at least one occasion it backfired.

Ed and Marion Young have a garden behind their home in New Haven, Vermont. The garden is handy to the local woods, and a trio of raccoons made nightly visits to the plot as well as to the nearby compost pile.

They had been welcome guests so far. However, the sweet corn was fast becoming ripe. Raccoons like corn the way bears like honey, and a family of them can reduce the whole crop to leftovers in a single night. So Ed put up a low electric fence where it'd warn them to keep their distance.

"Those three raccoons visited the compost heap first, as usual," he told me. "Then they took off on the path toward the garden, single file. The first one hit that hot wire with its nose and jumped back. Raccoon Number Two thought he'd been attacked, and bounced into Number Three. The result was the biggest free-for-all you ever saw."

So, as one of my biology professors once told us, "*E pluribus* —except when *unum*." Or, if you prefer: "Stick together, boys: every man for himself."

Resourceful wild animals of many kinds have learned to get along with us and our ways—barring such gadgetry as electric fences. Many people who have visited Yosemite or Yellowstone have met those famous bears. These creatures do the rounds of the camp sites for edibles and often cause "bear jams" on the roads as they stop cars for a handout. Ground squirrels and marmots do the same in other parks. An Eastern version occurs with each arriving car at Gifford Woods State Park near Rutland, Vermont. There the performer is a northern gray squirrel.

No crumbs or potato chips for this squirrel, however. It greets the incoming cars, yes—but not the people. What it seeks is on the front of each car: the insects that have been crushed against the radiator. For some reason it has abandoned the prosaic diet of nuts and seeds and has appointed itself a combined sanitation and welcoming committee.

Another rodent took a different tack when it came to campers. This one paid a visit to Hank and Thea Zablocki. An extended visit, as it turned out.

Somehow, when the Zablockis packed their car in New Jersey for a trip to Canada, they included a white-footed mouse. "When we stopped the first night in New York State," Thea told me, "the children saw it by the picnic table. We thought it belonged there."

"But then we began to suspect something on our second

150   RONALD ROOD

night out," Hank added. "Some of our food showed definite signs of mice. When we saw the mouse twice in Canada we were sure: we had a passenger."

The family wasn't about to oust a mouse hundreds of miles from home. Besides, it was sort of fun to think of it, riding along and seeing the world by shock absorber, as it were. So they wrapped their food securely and continued their trip.

On their way they stopped at our house, which was where I learned of their small stowaway. "And we still have it," said Hank, holding out a nibbled cookie. "We bought these cookies just yesterday, and this is what the mouse did last night. It's been with us more than a week."

We marveled at the wanderlust that possessed such a tiny creature. We also marveled at the timing that allowed it to leave the car at each camp site, forage around, and get aboard again before departure. How did it know a camp site from a supermarket parking lot, say, or a highway rest stop?

Perhaps the answer lay in the whitefoot's nocturnal habits. The little tyke merely remained in place all day and came out at night—in this case, while the family slept at a campground. Then, with dawn, it went back to its berth.

On the final lap of the trip its luck ran out. The Zablockis arrived at their destination well after dark. Somewhere along the line, perhaps when they paused at a restaurant at dusk, the mouse must have left the car. Possibly a stray cat got it, or perhaps the car drove off while the mouse was investigating a gum wrapper. At any rate, when the Zablockis carefully unpacked the next day, there was no sign of the little traveler.

Two days later, Hank decided to clean the trunk and put away the camping supplies for another year. Then they discovered the reason for the tiny rodent's persistence in accompanying them throughout the long journey. There, in the spare tire well, was a fluffy nest the size of a softball. It was made of material pulled from the rear of the seat cushions. Curled in the nest was one little dead baby.

The mouse had been a mother who had chosen the car trunk as a place to have her young just before the trip. When the nursery suddenly developed wheels she had no choice but to go along. Then, with that single baby to help tie her to her unorthodox dwelling, she bravely sought her food in new surroundings every night.

White-footed mice are forever getting into scrapes. Perhaps that's a sign of their individuality. While they spend much of the summer in the woods and brushland, these deer mice, as they are also called, yield to the lure of a warm, fragrant house in the fall. A single mouse may tote as much as a gallon of maple seeds, cherry pits and sunflower seeds to some favored spot. You suddenly realize it has moved in when you pull a book off the shelf and a pint of pits cascades out onto the floor. Or—as happened with the creaky typewriter I'm using to compose these words—you go to hammer away and the keys won't work. One look and you discover that the machine's innards have become a basket of birdseed.

One time I placed several aluminum trays of pumpkin and squash seed to dry on top of a filing cabinet. I nibble on the seeds all winter, plant the remainder in spring. In searching for something in the files, I pulled out all of those heavy drawers—and promptly tipped the whole affair over.

When I righted the cabinet, the top drawer was a mess.

RONALD ROOD

The papers were still in place, but those flat seeds had filtered halfway down into dozens of folders. Pressed for time at the moment, I slammed the file shut in frustration, hastily swept up, and left the room.

Several days later I went to use the file. Remembering the seeds, I expected the worst as I pulled open that top drawer. But not a seed was to be seen.

A white-footed mouse had explored the upstairs of our old farmhouse in those few days. Poking into the back of the file cabinet, it had audited my records. There, in the dark, it had extracted every seed. For the rest of the winter we were reminded of the upset file cabinet: pumpkin seeds in slippers, coat pockets, and behind the cushion of my easy chair. Even now, two years later, I'm not sure we've found them all.

The outsized curiosity of these dark-eyed rodents with the big ears takes them almost anywhere. Experienced owners of vacation camps turn all deep buckets and wastebaskets over when they leave for the winter, otherwise there'll be dead mice in them next year. Peg's mother found a bureau drawer stuffed with tatters of old stockings when she opened her cottage for the summer. The drawer had apparently been a mousery through the winter.

A vacationing friend turned on the gas stove in her mountain cabin here in Lincoln—and promptly ignited a whitefoot nest near the burner. The mother almost became a living torch as she tried to rescue her quartet of youngsters.

Not always are rodents tied that close to home. One Christmas vacation George, a gerbil, escaped from his combination of boxes and tunnels on the sink in Peg's kindergarten classroom. The door was open so he made his way into the hall. From there he could go to the rest of the school. The custodian, feeling it was his fault that George got away, quietly tried to catch him before Peg returned. He put out tempting bits of apple, seeds, and humane live traps in several likely places, but to no avail. The little fellow ignored them.

When Peg got back from vacation, the custodian, crushed,

admitted his defeat. But my wife was not the least disturbed. She merely put the gerbil's apartment house down on the floor. She supplied fresh food, opened the hatch where he'd escaped, and left it overnight.

"I figure the grass looked greener down the hall for George when he first wandered off," she told me that evening. "But maybe he's reconsidered. Once you're away, the grass begins to look pretty good right back home, too."

Apparently George agreed. Surrounded by the cardboard he'd cut into bits, the sunflower hulls he'd piled in one corner and the shreds of newspaper he'd fashioned into a nest, he was back in his old haunts the next morning.

Opportunity came at the same instant to a man and a wild animal in a Canadian Provincial Park one summer evening. The man was a park ranger. The animal was a—well, let him tell it.

"I was 'way off in the back country," the ranger informed us. "I'd left the Jeep around a bend in the road and was returning to it when I saw a dog sniffing at the tires. But when I looked closer I realized it wasn't a dog at all. It was a full-grown red fox."

While the animal was busy, the man eased himself closer. "That fox investigated all four of the tires," he continued. "When he got to the last one he added his own 'signature,'

RONALD ROOD

just like a dog. And while he was about that little bit of business he looked up and spotted me."

The ranger chuckled. "You never saw such a surprised fox in your life. He stood there like a statue with his leg cocked up in the air. Then, apparently remembering what he was doing, he gave a defiant last little jet and lowered the leg to the ground.

"I figured he was getting ready to run, so I spoke to him, kind of quiet. 'Here, boy,' I said, 'want to play?' "

As he uttered these words to Peg and me, the ranger slowly stooped down and picked up a twig. "I bent over and got a stick," he said. "Then I flipped it to him—like this. And darned if that fox didn't grab it."

The next scene must have been a delight. "The fox ran around and around in the road—up and down, just like a playful dog. He tossed the stick in the air, caught it, dropped it and picked it up again. And all the time that beautiful tail was waving with so much grace. He was still playing when he ran off into the woods. It was one of the prettiest pictures I've ever seen."

An event just as appealing once happened to the naturalist Alan Devoe. Devoe was ambling through the woods when he saw a small animal approaching. As he stood and waited, he realized it was a tiny fawn.

The little creature, only a few hours old, wobbled right up to him before it saw him. Then it stood stock still.

On the spur of the moment, the naturalist put forth his hand. Extending a finger, he offered it to the fawn, just as one might give a finger or two to a newborn calf to suck.

Likewise on the spur of the moment, the fawn received the offering. It sucked on the finger just as it would on its mother's teat.

Then, suddenly, the little creature stopped. Its eyes widened as the extent of its folly apparently began to sink in. Here was a helpless baby rashly accepting the advances of a huge,

unknown creature. The realization was too much: the fawn collapsed.

Alan Devoe quietly withdrew, hoping the youngster would forget about the incident when it revived. And most likely it did: along with the impulsive behavior of animals seems to go an ability to live for each moment. Thus they escape two of the largest worries that plague human beings: the past and the future.

That small deer hadn't had time to find what the world was about. Yet there's a native intelligence that seems to guide animals where experience is lacking. Perhaps it's opportunity knocking again, but in a different form. Even centuries of domestic ease may not erase it. Take the case of the two little pigs.

The two pigs were in a pen belonging to Brenda and John Ladue. The pen was on a tiny plateau above the New Haven River.

Ordinarily the pen would be well away from the water, but a series of late-summer rains had swollen the feeder streams, and the river was a torrent. Overflowing its banks, it crept toward the pigs' enclosure.

"We looked at them in the afternoon," Brenda Ladue said. "But the river didn't seem to be coming any higher, so we decided they'd be all right."

As luck would have it, however, a thunderstorm built up late in the day and a cloudburst descended on the town. The river boiled and roared, but the Ladues never thought of the pigs until well after dark. "Then when we realized we'd forgotten them we ran out through the mud, expecting to see them drowned, or washed away," Brenda said.

And how had the little pigs fared in the flood? "Better'n we had any idea they would," John Ladue said. "When they saw the water rising, they did something you'd never think would happen. They pushed the dirt in their pen over toward the flooded side and made a little dam. Of course the dam didn't work, because the water flowed around the ends. So they were wet up to the belly when we rescued them. They were soaked—but at least they'd tried."

It is creatures like these that keep this old Underwood exercising nearly every day. Just as it's more fun to go to a concert, say, when you're with someone else, it multiplies my pleasure to share these animals with you. An ermine-coated weasel which once followed me through the crunchy snow on a bitter January night made our walk that much more of an event because I've told you about it here. So is the two-day battle between an Argiope spider—whose body is as big as a green grape—and a foot-long garter snake (now which one would *you* root for?). It was declared a draw when the entangling web gave way on the third morning in an extra-heavy dew. So, too, is the spectacle of a large dog fleeing in panic from the woods with an infuriated doe at its heels. Such a performance, I believe, says plenty about mother love.

The Happy Equation   157

To tell of the plants and animals that are so much a part of my world thus gives me half the pleasure I get from making their acquaintance—even if the story sometimes gets a little garbled. Consider a small friend of mine and her encounter with a honeybee.

My youthful friend is the niece of Bob and Betty Douglas, whom you've met earlier in these pages. Small Betsy Douglas was visiting Bob's orchard one day and admiring the apple blossoms. Around her buzzed scores of honeybees. Their hives had been brought into the orchard especially for pollination, and they were hard at work on that balmy day. Betsy went to pick a blossom that was occupied by a bee, and the indignant insect stung her.

Betsy burst into tears. The tears were not so much from the pain, though, as from the knowledge that a bee dies after it uses its sting. The barbed lance, she had learned, remains stuck in the victim. Thus, when the bee is brushed off, portions of its internal organs are torn away.

Grief-stricken, Betsy made her way to the owner of the hives. "I killed one of your bees," she confessed. "How much do I owe you?"

To share such events is for me a privilege. Especially so if I can tell you a story or two about ordinary creatures that figure in extraordinary tales. Of course, some of these fancy yarns may not be quite what they seem. Witness, for example, my friend Al and his clandestine dinner.

At least I'll call him Al. He lives in a remote region well beyond the pale of the warden and the game laws. A marsh near his home always produces a duck or a goose. Al takes only what he requires for food, in season or out " . . . Although I only take the drakes in nesting season. That way I figure I don't make any orphans, Ron."

One autumn day a flotilla of Canada geese landed on the marsh. It was not yet hunting season, but Al bagged a goose anyway. When he retrieved it, he discovered that it bore a leg band. The instructions said to return the band to the U.S. Fish and Wildlife Service. In response, the Service would send a full report to the person who found it.

Al was curious about that band. Nevertheless, he hesitated to send it in before hunting season: there might be questions. So he put it up on the shelf, intending to mail it in a few weeks.

Time passed, and the band was forgotten. The weeks stretched into months, the months into years. Then, eleven years after Al and his wife had enjoyed that goose dinner, they moved to another house.

"When my wife was packing the kitchen things," Al told me, "she found the goose band. It said *Send to Fish and Wildlife Service* on it, so she mailed it in."

He chuckled at the thought. "Bigosh, it seems that her letter had hardly got into the mail before she had a reply. Airmail and everything. 'Congratulations,' it said. 'You have just helped establish a new record for long life in the Canada goose!' "

No, figures don't lie. They just don't always tell the truth, that's all.

Even the words in a book, careful as I may be in putting them down, may not give the complete story. Dorothy Ulsamer, a writer friend of mine, pointed out this problem in a letter:

"Once I made the mistake [she wrote] of taking my sister on one of my walks to where I knew certain wildflowers were blooming . . . the marsh marigold and the wild lily-of-the-valley. I'm used to ducking through brambles, jumping over streams, trudging for miles up hill and down vale. Gamely she followed. When I finally slid down the final hill and held some brush aside for her to see the particular flower I was after, she sat there, a huge mosquito bite on one cheek, her hair a damp mess and her legs quivering with fatigue, and said, 'It sounds so much easier in your stories.' "

One last comment. It wraps up my thoughts about animals, and about writing. It also includes those wonderful neighbors who helped me begin this book and who should help me finish it. It was at a library meeting in Montpelier, and the hostess had just introduced me to a friend of hers.

The friend considered my name for a moment. Then she brightened. "Oh," she said, "I know you! You're the man who writes all the nature books!"

"No, ma'am," I admitted. "Not *all* of them."

Hardly. But with her help—and an assist from a virtual Noah's Ark from mice to elephants—I'll try to do my share.

RONALD ROOD

Index